Praise for Flex

This book is a must-read, with great exampl
and practical strategies that help leaders to 'reset' and thrive at work.

Brooke Young, Director, Young Consulting Group

Karen has a way of articulating and simplifying the overwhelming,
self-sabotaging thoughts, feelings and behaviours that plague even the
most stoic of leaders. Refreshingly practical and gently encouraging,
FlexAbility is a must-read for any leader looking for a pragmatic, reassuring,
positive and immediately executable playbook for everyday success.

Amanda Kramer, Head of Marketing, Homely.com.au

FlexAbility couldn't be arriving at a better time for so many in our communities.
The long-term drain on resilience for so many around us has been significant.
To change our environment starting with ourselves is key, and *FlexAbility*
provides useful and well thought through approaches and activities to move
forward, as we chart a path from the interim normal of today to a future
where hope and optimism fills the gaps of uncertainty and anxiety.

**Mike Schneider, Chair, Love Me Love You; Board Member, Corporate
Mental Health Alliance Australia; Managing Director, Bunnings Group**

This is such a relevant and helpful guide to 2022 and beyond! The current
working environment is full of traps – we are always on, but expectations
feel higher than ever, and we risk achieving less and feeling less purposeful.
It seems counterintuitive – if not blasphemous - to think that we can become
more effective and more at peace with ourselves, but *FlexAbility* provides
a guide that will help every business leader be more aware of their
wellbeing and effectiveness.

Duncan Phillips, Chief Executive UK & Ireland, IVC Evidensia

In this hyper-relevant book for today's world of work, *FlexAbility* provides
high-performing leaders with a comprehensive and pragmatic guide to
protecting wellbeing by learning to influence what matters most. Dr Morley
deftly combines research with real-life stories to bring to life the challenges of
leading during a pandemic, along with the solutions for doing so successfully.

Dr Kelly Windle, Vice-President Organisation Capability, Bluescope

The intense disruption of the past two years has placed significant and untold demands on leaders across all organisations. *FlexAbility* couldn't be timelier. It provides valuable, evidence-based insights into the challenges faced by us all, together with accessible and practical advice to help us identify what matters to each of us, as well as clear guidance to enable us to reimagine and reshape our lives for the future and for the better.

Diana Vernon, Principal, Methodist Ladies College, Melbourne

FlexAbility is an outstanding piece of work. Living a 'rich, purpose-filled life, doing meaningful work, while prioritising your wellbeing' is within everyone's grasp. I wish I'd written this work. It is a game-changer.

Mark Butler, Clinical Psychotherapist

I thoroughly recommend this book. It is engaging and highly relevant to today's working pressures when so many I know are exhausted. The evidence-based approach, coupled with practical examples and rich and thought-provoking content, really help develop a more personal sense of how to achieve direction, change and balance. Finally, a book that offers practical and relevant advice about how to bring direction, change and balance back to working life.

Dr Jessica Triay, Clinical Unit Head Endocrinology, Bendigo Health

FlexAbility should be the essential guide for leaders on how to turn around burnout. Reset and recovery will become the way of surviving the increasingly demanding workplace we find ourselves in, and this book is the blueprint for ensuring we, and the organisations we work for, survive.

Kerrie Akkermans, CEO, Girl Guides South Australia

I found this book to be one of the most refreshing self-help books that I have read in a very long time. The concept of flexAbility is simple yet life changing in a world where we all have to navigate and find our own new work-life balance. This much-needed book supports workplace change, together with empowering the highly motivated professional with easy, usable tools.

Dr Tina Soulis, Founder & Director, Alithia Life Sciences

What a timely analysis and valuable tool *FlexAbility* is, packed full of useful insights and support for high-achieving leaders in today's working environment. After working with Karen for a number of years, it's no surprise that she's developed such a clear, compelling and practical guide for leaders.

Emily Phillips, Manager Regional Services, Melbourne Water

Karen Morley

Flex Ability

HOW HIGH ACHIEVERS
BEAT BURNOUT AND FIND FREEDOM
IN AN OVERWORKED WORLD

MAJOR
STREET

MAJOR STREET First published in 2022 by Major Street Publishing Pty Ltd
info@majorstreet.com.au | +61 421 707 983 | majorstreet.com.au

© Karen Morley 2022
The moral rights of the author have been asserted.

 A catalogue record for this book is available
NATIONAL from the National Library of Australia
LIBRARY
OF AUSTRALIA

Printed book ISBN: 978-1-922611-24-6
Ebook ISBN: 978-1-922611-25-3

Cover design by Tess McCabe
Internal design by Production Works
Printed in Australia by Ovato, an Accredited ISO AS/NZS 14001:2004
Environmental Management System Printer.

10 9 8 7 6 5 4 3 2 1

CONTENTS

INTRODUCTION

'[M]y life feels… [l]ike time confetti – one big, chaotic hurst of exploding slivers, bits and scraps.' – Brigid Schulte[1]

Let's face it, overwork seems here to stay. The promise of a post-pandemic 'reset' that would reduce the pace of work for knowledge workers, and make flexible work practices mainstream, has a hollow ring to it. Instead, life feels even more like time confetti.

Rather than COVID-19's remote work experiment creating a 'great reset',[2] expectations of overwork have increased. Feelings of anxiety have intensified. Burnout has blown out to the extent that more workers experience it than not.

I know that I fell for the 'great reset'. Three to six months after the start of the pandemic, I thought that we were heading for a fundamental rethink about how, when and where we work. There seemed so much promise.

We'd pivoted to remote work in record time. Years of difficulties and false starts in trying to increase flexibility and encourage working from home were overturned overnight. Commutes were slashed, freeing up swathes of time.

Organisations successfully functioned from individuals' homes. And not just a few workers and not just intermittently – entire workforces, for months.

We learned that remote work could be done.

Two years into the pandemic, however, some CEOs are still hellbent on getting everyone back into the office. They believe that the office is the only place where productive work happens. Some say that flexibility compromises the company's culture, even though their employees, when asked, say they want to work flexibly. It's flexibility that's at risk of being compromised.

It seems like a case of the more things change, the more they stay the same. The remote work pivot has shown, in particular, just how fundamental overwork is to modern workplaces. To show up to do a 'normal' day's work isn't enough; neither is showing up today to do the same amount of work you did yesterday.

As Rahaf Harfoush writes in her book *Hustle and Float,* modern management principles are faulty:

> *'Frederick Winslow Taylor was actually fired by Bethlehem Steel for failing to produce tangible results. It turned out that after a brief spike in performance, forcing workers to produce more in less time exhausted them to the point that their overall productivity was damaged in the long run.'*[3]

Taylorism didn't work in factories on production lines and it's even less suited to modern knowledge work. Yet we remain trapped in the pursuit of ever more work and ever more productivity. Even the challenges of a global pandemic haven't changed that!

What powers this pursuit? Leaders who are ambitious, competitive and overconfident. They chase continuous growth, seek ever larger rewards and drive overwork. They're prepared to sacrifice everything to win the game.

Leaders who are high-achieving, conscientious and agreeable get caught in the slipstream. Avery is one such leader, and her work ethic and need for achievement mean that she sets her standards high. She's considered to have high potential and be ready for promotion, but she's hesitant to take that step. She sees the C-suite executives in her organisation working incredibly long hours, with heavy demands on their time; they embody 'always on'.

Avery's not a machine: she's a human. She has a partner, two kids and a dog. Her father, who lives an hour away, was recently diagnosed with early onset dementia. Life is full; she works full-time and flexibly, working her five days in four to be able to balance her family needs and work demands.

At her best, when she's purposeful, focused and influential, Avery feels on top of her game; work gives her a surge of energy. Her organisation and colleagues love working with her: she's invited to participate in many projects, to give advice and support others. She exemplifies the old adage – 'If you want something done, give it to a busy person'.

Avery is ripe for overwork. As a high achiever, she sets tough personal standards and enjoys meeting them. Her conscientiousness translates into a high work ethic, and she takes her performance and output seriously. As a highly agreeable leader, she is willing to do what it takes.

But there's a tipping point, and it's not always easy to notice it. When the pressure builds, Avery does too much, cares too much and tries too hard. Chronic stress and burnout loom. Avery's thinking fractures; she's burdened by others' emotional needs. She starts to doubt herself, make mistakes and feel like a fraud. Surely this would only be worse at a more senior level?

This is what overwork does to amazing people. An organisational context of overwork sets the pace, and high-achieving leaders are readily drawn into its vortex.

In a world where overwork remains an expectation for knowledge workers, flexible work is a pipedream. No matter how flexibly

Avery works, whether from home or the office, whether she can choose when she starts and finishes is pretty much irrelevant given the expectation of overwork that she faces daily. No matter how she manages these variables, she'll still overwork.

What should leaders like Avery do? If her organisation isn't one of the few which are taking overwork seriously (no matter their flexible work policies), then Avery needs to reset herself. A personal reset might not change the bigger picture, but Avery can't afford to wait around for that to happen. She needs a better way to navigate her world, and she needs it now.

The heart of her new focus should not be flexibility – where and when she works – it's what I call 'flexAbility' – why and how she works.

Flexibility is how the system operates; organisations grant workers certain freedoms in relation to their work location and working hours. Flexibility is often associated with part-time work, even though part-time workers often overwork. It tends to put limits on career progress: if you want to work flexibly, you may be judged as lacking true dedication to work.

FlexAbility is how you operate in this demanding system. It's the freedom you grant yourself to avoid the sacrifices of overwork and live a rich, purpose-filled life, doing meaningful work while prioritising your wellbeing. Much of my coaching is focused on helping leaders like Avery and others profiled throughout the book (using pseudonyms) to be more flexAble.

If you know why you do what you do and where work fits into your sense of purpose, you can better align your work practices to suit. If you have good methods for focusing on the work that matters most, you are more likely to achieve your goals and aspirations. Without a clear sense of purpose, however, you'll forever be swept up in the whirlwind of 'too much to do and not enough time to do it in' – always catching up, not being your best and facing down another bout of burnout.

This book is designed for the Averys of the world, to help you create your own oasis of calm amid the whirlwind. It has three parts:

1. Know what matters.
2. Do what matters.
3. Influence what matters.

Part I, 'Know what matters', focuses on you. Chapter 1 provides an outline of what overwork, stress and burnout do to you, and how you can protect your wellbeing. Chapter 2 helps you to find and live your purpose and Chapter 3 focuses on psychological flexibility – flexible thinking, feeling and learning.

Part II, 'Do what matters', helps you to recalibrate your work to make it easy to do what matters most. Chapter 4 helps you to rediscover the love in your work, Chapter 5 helps you to deepen your focus and Chapter 6 helps you to make good work habits stick.

Part III, 'Influence what matters', then helps you to review and reset your influence. Chapter 7 helps you to flex your style so that influencing others is easier and more effective, Chapter 8 helps you to delegate more and Chapter 9 helps you to increase your influence and impact.

Every chapter contains an assessment exercise to help you identify where you might make improvements, and also a 'reset' exercise – a set of actions to take.

When you know what matters, do what matters and influence what matters, you can be flexAble. You can better defend against the demands of overwork, stop taking on too much, feel greater freedom and enjoy your life more. You might still work long hours, but you'll know why you do. Your mind won't feel pulled in so many different directions that time feels like confetti. You will feel composed, vital, focused and free to be the influential leader you aspire to be.

PART I

Know what matters

There's 'a silver lining… to the pandemic:
the opportunity to make work lives more purposeful,
productive, agile, and flexible'.

LYNDA GRATTON[4]

OVERWORK CREATES a whirlwind of continuous, competing demands. It makes it hard to focus, to identify what's most important, and to switch off and enjoy your leisure time. While the pandemic hasn't liberated us from the reality of overwork, it has, as Lynda Gratton says, provided impetus for resetting ourselves. When you know what matters, what you need to do to reset yourself becomes clearer.

In this part of the book, Chapter 1 starts with what's at the core: you and your wellbeing! The chapter defines what stress and burnout are and how they erode your time, energy and health. The assessment exercise in this chapter will help you take stock of your wellbeing and burnout levels: you need to make sure overwork doesn't compromise your health. The chapter's reset exercise is a five-step process to recharge and renew yourself.

Making your life more purposeful doesn't just make you feel better, it also helps you live longer. Chapter 2 explains what purpose is and how it casts its magic, and provides you with a series of tools to clarify your purpose. Along with purpose, clarifying your values, identity, aspiration and goals will help you to make your life more intentional. With this clarity, it's much easier to make work choices that prevent overwork and allow you to fulfil your purpose and find freedom.

The final focus for Part I is on psychological flexibility – flexible thinking, feeling and learning – a superpower for achieving flexAbility. Even smart high achievers sometimes make the wrong choices, feel lousy about themselves and repeat old mistakes. Chapter 3 helps you to avoid getting stuck in unhelpful thoughts and rise above the dilemmas and barriers you face. It shows you how to avoid feeling too emotionally caught up, to avoid caring *too* much. It encourages you to prioritise curiosity to increase your learning.

When you know what matters, you are freer to make better choices that serve your purpose. That generates rather than saps your energy, and allows you to feel aligned, accomplished and satisfied.

CHAPTER 1

START WITH YOU

Companies make burnout more likely for top performers
by putting them on the hardest projects, using them to
compensate for weaker team members and to help out
on efforts not related to their work. – Matt Plummer[5]

Avery reached the end of the second major COVID-19 lockdown expecting to feel a huge surge of relief. Instead, she felt overwhelming fatigue, accompanied by a degree of cynicism and lack of interest that took her by surprise.

When the pandemic began, Avery had been concerned to protect and support her largely field-based teams. She'd wanted them to know that they were her priority. She'd swung into action quickly to get on top of the many changes, risks and issues so that she could provide clear guidance to them.

Avery was prepared to do whatever it took – and not just at work. At home, she shared schooling responsibilities with her partner and provided support to her parents.

The cycle of lockdowns and uncertainty meant continual rework and redesign. Avery's time was consumed by 'work about the work' and rework, which became dispiriting.

Under normal circumstances, she worked hard and coped with a lot of pressure. With the added uncertainties and increased working hours required to respond to COVID-19, she realised she'd hit the wall. She was burned out.

In a work context of unrelenting demands, the ceaseless quest for increased productivity and the heightened uncertainty of a pandemic, it is not surprising to find an increased incidence of stress and burnout, particularly among high-achievers.

In this chapter, I'll discuss what stress and burnout are and how they differ. I'll explain the connection between overwork and the increased prevalence of stress and burnout. Even top performers like Avery – who enjoy the challenges of complex knowledge work and have a strong work ethic – succumb to it. The chapter then outlines a five-step process for minimising stress and burnout and prioritising your renewal.

Even before the pandemic, burnout was said to be reaching 'epic proportions';[6] a third of workers reported that they felt burned out. Since the pandemic, anxiety and burnout have skyrocketed. UK research[7] shows that levels of distress in the community doubled in 2020. The rate of mental distress in the Australian community was 2.5 times[8] the rate before the pandemic.

The impact in the US[9] was higher still, with an increase to almost 40 per cent of adults reporting symptoms of anxiety or depression. A global study by Asana[10] indicated that nearly four in five knowledge workers in Australia and almost nine in ten in the US were feeling burned out.

Asana claims that mid-pandemic, a mere 26 per cent of time is spent on meaningful work and 14 per cent on forward-looking strategy. Sixty per cent is spent 'working on work'. Changes include a longer working day, an increase in unnecessary meetings, duplication of work and a lack of clarity about tasks and roles.

In the study of workers reported in *The Australian Workforce Response to COVID-19*,[11] 55 per cent of respondents said their main cause of stress was change to ways of working. The biggest changes were working with technology, blurred boundaries, time management and worry about the future.

People have had highly varied responses to the changes COVID-19 has brought to our working lives. For some, working from home provided a respite from a long commute and meant extra time available. For others, it was harder to maintain the boundary between work and home, particularly when home became home, work *and* school.

As time goes on, it's clear there will be continuing waves of lock-downs, restrictions and new pandemic-related crises. To date, employees have been sprinting, going above and beyond, and that just can't be sustained. Stress and anxiety help us to respond to the challenges we face, and most people experience manageable levels of worry and anxiety, even during crises. But when the challenges don't let up, stress goes beyond manageable levels.

As a McKinsey article[12] pointed out in November 2020, we are in for a protracted period of pandemic fatigue. We'll see more disillusionment, grief and exhaustion: all fodder for burnout. We need to become better at noticing stress and anxiety, and to reduce overwork, increase wellbeing at work and increase self-care.

Assess your stress and burnout

When Avery felt like she was hitting the wall, it was time to take stock. Here are two assessments, one on burnout and one on wellbeing, to help you do the same.

The burnout assessment questions are based on the gold-standard work of Christina Maslach and Michael Leiter.[13] They provide a starting point from which to consider your own potential for burnout.

Burnout assessment

Over the last month or so, how often have you felt:	All of the time	Most of the time	More than half the time	Less than half the time	Some of the time	At no time
1. Exhausted?	5	4	3	2	1	0
2. Cynical about work?	5	4	3	2	1	0
3. Resentful of others?	5	4	3	2	1	0
4. Professionally ineffective?	5	4	3	2	1	0
5. Disengaged from your work?	5	4	3	2	1	0
6. That you need to work less?	5	4	3	2	1	0

Each question addresses an aspect of burnout. A score of 3 or more on any one question is concerning. A score of 3 or more on two or more questions may be indicative of burnout. If your pattern of scores is of concern to you, I recommend you seek assistance from an appropriately qualified professional.

Next, complete the WHO-5,[14] following. It's a subjective measure of general wellbeing, extensively used in global research and clinical settings. This is an additive scale: answer each question, add the scores for the five items, then multiply by four to convert it to a percentage score.

WHO-5 assessment

Please indicate for each of the five statements which is closest to how you have been feeling over the past two weeks.	All of the time	Most of the time	More than half the time	Less than half the time	Some of the time	At no time
1. I have felt cheerful and in good spirits.	5	4	3	2	1	0
2. I have felt calm and relaxed.	5	4	3	2	1	0
3. I have felt active and vigorous.	5	4	3	2	1	0
4. I woke up feeling fresh and rested.	5	4	3	2	1	0
5. My daily life has been filled with things that interest me.	5	4	3	2	1	0

The general population mean score is 70. If your score is 50 or lower, I recommend you seek assistance from an appropriately qualified professional, such as a general practitioner or psychologist, or reach out to your organisation's Employee Assistance Program.

Avery's WHO-5 score gave her pause for thought; she realised just how seldom she had enjoyed those positive feelings lately.

Take some time to reflect on your scores from the two assessments, using the following questions:

1. What areas, if any, concern you?
2. What tools or practices do you currently find effective to help relieve stress and burnout?
3. What tools or practices do you find are most effective to help improve your wellbeing?
4. What areas do you find most difficult to change?
5. What do you need to prioritise?

How to recognise stress

At the core of wellbeing and burnout is our response to stressors. We automatically respond to stressful situations with a fight-or-flight response. This is a highly adaptive response that our bodies have perfected over tens of thousands of years, and it serves to protect us from harm. Before modern times, when we faced a threat such as a wild animal on the savannah, our stress response meant that we ran from the threat before we'd even consciously decided to do so, and we probably set a personal best time as well!

It's helpful to understand how the fight-or-flight response works. In response to a threat, our sympathetic nervous system (SNS) is automatically activated to prepare us to avoid the threat. The SNS comprises a network of brain structures, nerves and hormones. Under threat, a surge of hormones boosts the body's alertness and heart rate, sending blood to the muscles, fresh oxygen to the brain and glucose into the bloodstream. We are primed for action.

Adrenaline is the first hormone surge, and it triggers the sweating, rapid heartbeat and short breaths that we associate with stress and anxiety. If the threat continues, a surge of cortisol follows to maintain the response. The SNS also increases sensory perception – pupils dilate so vision expands, and hearing becomes more acute – to focus on the threat. Our attention narrows to allow quick judgements to be made, seemingly without effort. Another part of the response is physical protection – blood thickens, which increases clotting in preparation for injury, and pain perception temporarily decreases.

When the threat has passed, the parasympathetic nervous system (PNS) comes into play, returning the body to 'normal', slowing blood pressure, breathing rate and hormone flow. From fight-or-flight, we return to rest-and-digest. The PNS response reverses the impact of stress by stimulating renewal. Oxytocin and vasopressin are released, replacing adrenaline and cortisol.[15] This improves the immune system, stimulates the growth of new neurons and improves cognitive functioning.

Only one system – the SNS or PNS – can be dominant at a time. A trigger, such as threat or its removal, signals the need to shift from one to the other. Together, the SNS and PNS comprise the autonomic nervous system.

In our modern working lives, we face fewer physical threats, such as wild animals on the savannah. Most of our stressors are social, and many that we experience in our daily lives are minor – an irritation at a traffic jam, rushing to get to the next meeting or forgetting where we saved a particular document. Fighting and fleeing tend not to serve us as well, even though our bodies continue to respond as if they did.

What are your social threat triggers?

You may have heard of the SCARF model, created by David Rock,[16] which outlines five major social stressors:

- **S – Status**, a loss of personal importance or social standing

- **C – Certainty**, not being able to predict what will happen, feeling uncertain
- **A – Autonomy**, losing a sense of control over your choices
- **R – Relatedness**, loss of personal connection, lack of interpersonal safety, exclusion
- **F – Fairness**, feeling you receive different treatment, lack of transparency, a sense of injustice.

Which of these generate your greatest threat response? Knowing your triggers can help you to manage your response to them.

In social settings, feeling threatened diminishes cognitive resources and reduces awareness of interpersonal signals, and we are more likely to make faulty judgements or respond defensively. Small stressors seem much larger. When working with others, we are more likely to try to avoid – to flee – these stressors than we are to fight them.

How much you are triggered by various threats will depend on how important an activity is to you, how much general uncertainty you are feeling and whether others are watching or evaluating you. Your SNS response might range from being very mild and brief to more intense and extended, and then may become chronic.

The more often stress is experienced, and the more stressors that cause it, the greater the potential for it to become chronic.

Richard Boyatzis and his colleagues suggest that because many of our social stressors are small, the arousal of the SNS is mild.[17] That sounds like it's good news; however, removal of the threat may be similarly small, and therefore it may not automatically activate the PNS for recovery. Our SNS may remain activated even when there is no threat, increasing the chance of chronic stress.

Anticipation also triggers our stress response. When we think about that big presentation coming up or the difficult performance conversation we need to have, our SNS is activated in the same way as it is when we give the presentation or have the conversation. This adds to the time that we feel stressed.

The focus of this chapter is on stressors associated with work. However, there are many other causes of stress in everyday life, such as disrupted sleep, arguing with a spouse or family member, getting stuck in traffic, being late for an appointment, being angry at a specific person, watching others yell or shout, or worrying about something that might not turn out well. Feelings of stress, anxiety and worry accumulate, whether the causes are personal or work-related.

We need stress to survive – adrenaline gets us going – yet we experience too many real and anticipated stressors that affect our wellbeing. Too much stress compromises our health, limits thinking, slows learning and reduces engagement.

The difference between stress and burnout

The term 'burnout' was first coined in the 1970s, when Herbert Freudenberger and Christina Maslach began writing about its prevalence among mental health workers.[18] More recently, it has been associated with a broader range of causes and applied across occupations.

In 2019, the World Health Organization (WHO) recognised burnout as an official diagnosis, but not, importantly, as a medical condition:

> *'Burn-out is a syndrome conceptualized as resulting from chronic workplace stress that has not been successfully managed. It is characterized by three dimensions:*
>
> *· feelings of energy depletion or exhaustion;*

- *increased mental distance from one's job, or feelings of negativism or cynicism related to one's job; and*
- *reduced professional efficacy.*

Burn-out refers specifically to phenomena in the occupational context and should not be applied to describe experiences in other areas of life.'[19]

In 2021 Maslach and Leiter[20] identified many issues with how organisations are using the term 'burnout', as well as how they're assessing it. Often the term is used as if it were interchangeable with 'exhaustion', which it's not. Burnout is the combination of exhaustion, increased cynicism or mental distance from work and reduced professional effectiveness described in the WHO definition. The three elements interact with each other: as you feel more worn out, you have less effort to contribute, which leaves you feeling less effective, contributing to increased burnout. Burnout affects mood, learning and memory.

Our example leader Avery identified very keenly with the downward spiral as she faced the prospect of ongoing cycles of lockdowns and changes in working arrangements.

Maslach and Leiter point out that burnout is not an individual health problem: the term was created to highlight workplace issues so as to encourage employers to support the health and wellbeing of their workforce.

Burnout reduces people's ambitions, aspirations and sense of worth, and it interferes with their engagement in their work. Maslach and Leiter identify a very useful continuum that contrasts the three dimensions of burnout with five levels of engagement:

1. **engaged** – positive in all three areas; that is, energetic not exhausted, optimistic not cynical and feeling professionally effective

2. **disengaged** – negative in the area of cynicism, but not exhausted or ineffective

3. **ineffective** – negative in professional efficacy only

4. **overextended** – negative in exhaustion only

5. **burned out** – negative in all three areas.

The evidence from Leiter and Maslach suggests that 10 to 15 per cent of employees fit the true burnout profile, and about 30 per cent are engaged. That leaves more than half of them disengaged, ineffective or overextended. Not burned out, but certainly stressed and with plenty of opportunity for improvement.

INSIGHT

Too much stress can kill you

Dedicated, highly motivated workers – particularly leaders and those in health and service industries – may put up with high levels of stress for long periods of time, experiencing chronic stress. Neuroscience research suggests that this has a compounding negative impact on brain structure and function as well as overall health.[21]

Compared with workers who have not experienced chronic stress, these workers showed a significant difference in the size of their amygdalae, which were comparatively enlarged. The amygdala is central to the fight-or-flight response; when we are faced with threat it is the amygdala that activates the SNS. The amygdala also governs emotional reactions, including fear and aggression, and the negative emotions associated with burnout.

Those who had experienced chronic stress and burnout had more difficulty controlling their emotional responses and greater thinning of the frontal cortex. The more stress, the more wear and tear on the brain, which leads to memory, attention and emotional difficulties.

Grey matter also reduces because of the neurotoxic changes associated with the stress response.

Burnout also seems to impact on the body's neuroendocrine system. When stress is chronic, cortisol remains in the bloodstream, affecting the immune system and memory. When cortisol levels remain too high for too long, the body downshifts to producing particularly low levels, which is called 'hypocortisolism'. It's almost as if the body's stress response system itself becomes burned out.

Hypocortisolism induces low-grade inflammation throughout the body, and that contributes to severe health problems including the build-up of plaque in coronary arteries. This significantly increases the risk of heart attacks.

An Israeli study focused on the routine health screening of workers found that those who scored in the top 20 per cent on burnout had a 79 per cent higher risk of a coronary heart disease diagnosis.[22] A WHO study released in May 2021 claimed that in 2016, 488 million workers were exposed to the risks of long hours and more than 745,000 people died that year from heart disease or stroke caused by overwork (working more than 55 hours a week).[23] Between 2000 and 2016, the number of deaths from heart disease due to overwork increased by 42 per cent and from stroke by 19 per cent. That's just the tip of the iceberg when it comes to the long-term consequences of too much stress at work.

There is some emerging research that indicates that these effects of chronic stress on the brain may be reversible, fortunately – by engaging in exercise specifically, as well as by increasing the frequency and variety of renewal activities.

Why burnout is an organisational responsibility

Burnout is caused by a mismatch between the person and their job. It might be a temporary mismatch or an ongoing one.

Burnout occurs when job demands are too high, the person has low control and the reward–effort ratio is out of balance.

Causes include:

- **excessive workload demands** – too much to do and not enough time to do it in, resources are inadequate, bosses are unsupportive
- **lack of control** – unrealistic expectations of what can be achieved, a lack of communication among team members, a lack of autonomy to make day-to-day decisions
- **inadequate reward** – lack of recognition, neglect, inadequate pay, lack of pleasure in the work
- **lack of community** – low social support, high conflict, negative interactions with bosses
- **lack of fairness** – a feeling that promotions or work and development allocations aren't equitable, cheating, lack of transparency
- **misalignment of values** – values conflicts, feeling misaligned with personal principles, feeling compelled to work unethically, personal aspirations are unrealised.[24]

Burnout and its components can persist over time. Feeling exhausted, cynical or professionally ineffective can also continue for some time without tipping over into burnout.

Leiter and Maslach[25] found that one factor that did commonly tip workers over into burnout, however, was a sense of workplace unfairness. If workers felt that decisions were not fair – for example, there was favouritism or cheating – they were more likely to be burned out a year later. On the plus side, those workers who experienced improvement in workplace fairness were able to increase their engagement.

One of the biggest contributors to stress and burnout at work is bad leadership, sometimes caused by toxic leadership and other times by leader incompetence, according to organisational psychologist Tomas Chamorro-Premuzic.[26]

To reduce burnout, reduce workplace stressors

To create a vital workforce, work standards should be realistic, workers should be given the resources they need, and they should be provided with a reasonable degree of autonomy. Leaders need to pay attention to how they engage with their teams, prioritising clear communication about expectations, acknowledging achievements and being fair.

In a meta-analysis of studies involving more than 25,000 workers, Christina Guthier and her colleagues found that when workers experiencing burnout were given more autonomy over their work and received support, their experience of stress decreased.[27]

Clear communication – keeping workers in the loop on important decisions – decreases cynicism and prevents a slide into exhaustion. The predictability of their work and the ability to use their skills stopped workers who were feeling ineffective from experiencing further symptoms.[28]

To counteract the effect of poor leadership and its contribution to stress and burnout, try the following:

1. Prevent rather than cure. When hiring, focus more on candidates' potential and emphasise learning and emotional intelligence.
2. Assess for flaws, not just strengths. Remove toxic leaders as soon as they are noticed, as toxicity spreads rapidly.
3. Dig below the surface: engage more deeply with people to find out more about their experiences. Resilient people

show up as engaged even when they are treated poorly,
so the problems of poor leadership may not be apparent
for some time.

4. Remember that boring can be better. Flamboyant,
charismatic leaders create unpredictability, which causes
stress. Don't be too enchanted by such leaders; look closely
at their track record and character before you promote
them.[29]

Making workplaces more collaborative by strengthening peer
relationships is another way to overcome the impact of poor
leadership and other stressors. Improving workplace civility
reduces burnout. Set clear standards for civil workplace
behaviour, encourage positive and collaborative relationships
and weed out troublemakers. Pay attention to others' emotional
needs and wellbeing, and encourage the expression of warmth,
kindness and generosity.

None of this is rocket science. We've known about the workplace
contributors to engagement and effective performance for some
time – and it's not just that during COVID-19 we went into
hyperdrive without paying enough attention to recharging.
Before the crisis, we paid insufficient attention to the skills and
workplace cultures that promote wellbeing, so many leaders and
high performers were on the tipping point of burnout even then.

**The solution to burnout lies in reducing
overwork, promoting a more human work culture,
strong proactive stress management and
emphasising recovery and renewal.**

Burnout won't go away without a change in work conditions.
Returning to 'normal' post-COVID-19 is not going to happen.

Stop stress and beat burnout

Here are five evidence-based ways to diminish the amount of stress and burnout you feel (see Figure 1); they'll help you to recover and restore your wellbeing:

1. Recognise your response.
2. Reappraise what's happening.
3. Regulate how you react.
4. Recharge often.
5. Ensure you experience frequent and varied renewal.

Figure 1: Five tools to stop stress and beat burnout

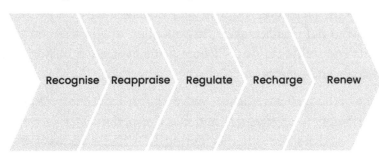

Recognise your body's response

Leadership researcher and award-winning author Robert E. Quinn and his colleagues suggest that having a good understanding of your body's stress response is a good place to start.[30] Understanding when the SNS kicks in and knowing what your body is doing helps you make sense of the situation and gives you a chance to decide what to do about it. The SNS might be automatic, but that doesn't mean that you can't change the effect it has.

Recognise the cues for your stress, referring to the social threat triggers identified by David Rock (listed on pages 17 and 18).

Reappraise your stress

If you can reappraise what is happening and see it in a positive light, you can help to reduce your stress. Recall your previous experiences of dealing successfully with the same triggers and reframe the situation in a more positive way based on those previous experiences. Then act on the reappraisal to move into a state you prefer.

Quinn suggests that a way to make this more powerful is to write down what happened in your previous experiences. You did it before; you can do it now. This is a great tactic designed to give you hope.

Regulate your reaction

Use self-regulation to connect to hope and to your higher sense of purpose, as this will trigger the PNS, helping your body to recover. The PNS response releases oxytocin, shifting you to a state of engagement and connection.

If you are feeling burned out, ask for help, even though this might be a little challenging if you are concerned about appearing inadequate. As Ron Carucci explains, though, good bosses will respect high achievers reaching out for help, might have noticed some signs of burnout already and will be prepared to take action to support you.[31] He suggests you start a conversation with your boss to evoke their empathy. Focus on the work as you explain what's going on. Take responsibility for the impact of your burnout, then appeal for help; try not to complain, and suggest solutions.

Wisely, Carucci counsels not to let the relief you feel from asking for help allow you to neglect the self-care that you need to do. You may feel a surge of energy from the conversation and the empathy you experience, but that is not enough!

If your boss is part of the problem, of course, reach out to others for support.

Recharge your energy

Resilience isn't so much about being able to endure more but about how, and how often, you recharge. The harder you work, the more recharging you need.

The basics of sleep, good nutrition and a regular exercise regime help you to manage your energy and are fundamental to wellbeing. They help you to maintain your 'charge' and to reduce your need to recharge.

To make sure you recharge during the day, take short breaks. Shift your attention, change work tasks, take short breaks when you feel your energy wane, go for a short walk, put your head on the desk for five minutes, or have a warm conversation with a friend or family member. Disengaging from your work recharges your energy. Rather than trying to keep pushing through your day and then using your leisure time to recover, recharge during the workday, even if you don't think you need it. That way, you'll feel less depleted at the end of the workday.

Recovery from the impact of stress at work is also facilitated by a deliberate process of detaching from work at the end of the day. The experience of detaching is associated with better self-reported mental and physical health, wellbeing and task performance.

There are five types of recovery experience that Sabine Sonnentag[32] and her colleagues identify:

1. **psychological detachment (by far the most powerful)** – disconnecting fully during non-work
2. **relaxation** – being free of tension and anxiety
3. **mastery and achievement**, including through learning

4. **control** – deciding what you will do, when and how

5. **enjoyment** – feeling pleasure.

Both recharging and detachment lower feelings of stress and burn-out. Make sure that you are investing in recharging throughout your day and in recovery at the end of the day. Having said that, there's a critical philosophical question to be asked about whether your leisure time should be framed as 'the time you recover from work'. Shouldn't it be the time you live your life? When you're feeling stressed or burned out, however, it's better than nothing.

Recharging is designed to reduce stress and decrease the chance of getting burned out, so that you are not using leisure time to recover from work. In Chapter 6, we'll explore how to make recharging a daily habit.

Promote renewal

Are your stress-management activities giving you the right experience? Experts in leadership and emotional intelligence Richard Boyatzis, Daniel Goleman and their colleagues advocate for intentionally activating the PNS to ameliorate the effects of stress and burnout.[33] They claim that recharging and recovery activities may not necessarily activate the PNS – for example, if you meditate but can't stop thinking about a problem while you're doing so, you're probably not activating the PNS. Pay attention to your state to make sure that you do experience renewal.

Ways to trigger the PNS include caring for others, caring for or playing with pets, having an enjoyable meal with family, volunteering, taking a nature walk, meditation, yoga, breathing exercises, purposeful reflection, laughter, spending quality time with partners and playing. Both frequency and variety in these activities are important. Variety is positively related to resilience and empathy and positively affects engagement, wellbeing and career satisfaction. Frequent renewal activities without variety (such as relying on meditation only) affects wellbeing but not engagement and career satisfaction.

Renewal is more comprehensive if there are not just more 'doses' of renewal activities per week, but also if they have greater variety.

A lower number and variety of renewal activities is significantly related to how much stress is experienced, and to feelings of depression and anxiety.

RESET YOUR STRESS

Whether or not you are able to control your workplace to prevent burnout, there are things that you can do for yourself to alleviate the impact of your context. These are all associated with being resilient and being able to endure setbacks with relative ease. They reduce your vulnerability to negative workplace features and help combat irritations and setbacks.[34]

Your wellbeing is critical to your effectiveness as a leader, as well as to increasing your freedom. Don't expect anyone else to prioritise it – use the five tools to put yourself first.

1. Recognise – notice when you are experiencing stress, even at low levels.

2. Reappraise – try to find a more positive way of framing the situation.

3. Regulate – think about successful past experiences you've had navigating this kind of situation.

4. Recharge – replenish your energy as it is consumed by detaching from work during the day and at the end of each day.

5. Renew – frequently engage in a variety of renewal activities.

CHAPTER 2

LIVE YOUR PURPOSE

'We're here to put a dent in the universe.
Otherwise why else even be here?' – Steve Jobs[35]

Marco had to admit that he didn't feel particularly fulfilled. At work, he was busy, and his leadership reputation was developing well. At home, his relationship with his wife seemed a little distant and he couldn't remember when he'd last read bedtime stories to his children, even though he was working from home.

He was shut in his office while family life went on around him. He was desperately trying to prioritise quality family time but knew he wasn't succeeding.

Marco was so busy just getting through the day-to-day of work that there never seemed to be time to focus on the people and things that mattered most to him. He had a vague sense of how he could put his dent in the universe but hadn't reflected on it lately. He figured that he'd just get over this spike of work, and surely then there would be time. But it wasn't happening.

While he was convinced that having a clearer purpose would help, it seemed a bit abstract and he wasn't quite sure how to go about it. With his purpose vague, Marco remained stuck, shut off from his family and unsatisfied with himself.

Perhaps the most important thing to be clear about to increase your leadership flexAbility is purpose. Why does being a flexAble leader matter to you? Because it helps you lead the life you want to lead, to be the person you want to be. With a clarity of purpose, you will be more motivated to protect your flexAbility.

To be flexAble, you need to fill your life with purpose; when purpose is your guide, everyday choices become easier. There are fewer decisions to make, because they have already been made: the course has been charted, and you can navigate along it. For Marco, being vague about his purpose and feeling dissatisfied with parts of his life meant that he was constantly making small decisions while avoiding some important ones. He was depleting his energy – not just by working long hours, but also by missing out on the significant health and wellbeing benefits that come from being clear about and aligned with purpose.[36]

This chapter will help you to reset your purpose. Why do you do what you do? Clarify that, then make work and life more meaningful, more intentional. Get clear about your purpose, your values, identity, aspiration and goals. This clarity doesn't just make flexAbility easier for you, it helps others to understand where you stand. If you say you want to lead flexAbly but then agree to everything that comes your way, you create confusion.

The clearer you are about your purpose, the clearer you can communicate why you do what you do, your choices and your reasons. When others understand you well, they are more likely to support you and help you to succeed. You will then increase your flexAbility, choosing what to do now and next based on what matters most to you.

Assess your purpose

How clear is your sense of purpose? The clearer it is, the better. It will change and adapt over time, but are you able to articulate it right now?

Assess your sense of purpose with the following agreement scale, which is adapted from the Purpose in Life subscale of the Ryff Psychological Wellbeing Scale.[37]

	Strongly disagree	Disagree	Neither agree nor disagree	Agree	Strongly agree
1. I enjoy making plans for the future and working to make them a reality.	1	2	3	4	5
2. I have a sense of direction and purpose in life.	1	2	3	4	5
3. I live life one day at a time and don't really think about the future.	5	4	3	2	1
4. I don't have a good sense of what it is I am trying to accomplish in life.	5	4	3	2	1

For items 1 and 2, 'Strongly agree' is the preferred result; for items 3 and 4, 'Strongly disagree' is the preferred result. Now reflect on your purpose in more detail:

1. How satisfied do you feel with your sense of purpose?
2. How do you revise and update your purpose?

3. What value might you get from having a clear/er purpose?

4. What's the next thing you need to do to clarify and confirm your purpose?

A framework for purpose

Being able to clearly articulate your purpose is inspiring, but it can take a bit of sweat to get there. Over my years of working with leaders to help them clarify and focus their purpose, I've found it helpful to use a structure that has several different yet related elements – values, aspiration, identity and goals. As shown in Figure 2, these elements help you make sense of your purpose and turn it into tangible action.

Figure 2: How to clarify your purpose

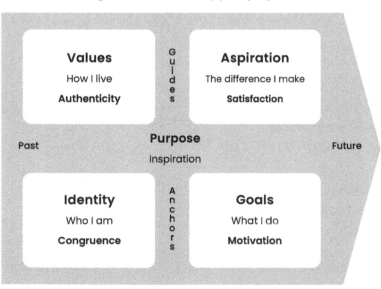

Your values and identity come from your past influences and experiences. Your aspiration and goals make meaning of your future. Values and aspirations are guides: they give direction about where you come from and where you want to go. Identity and goals, by contrast, are anchors, providing security and conviction as you grow and develop.

Purpose sits in the centre; it's both a guide and an anchor. While it's also about the past and the future, it holds its greatest power in the present, as it's in the present moment that we flexAbly manage ourselves to ensure we continue to live with purpose.

Values are shaped by past experiences and define how you wish to live your life. They are strongly associated with purpose: clarify which values you live by now and which you want to live by into the future. It's the difference between looking through a grimy, blurry windscreen and a sparkling, clear one that lets you see your way ahead.

Living in alignment with your values is key to feeling authentic. The better your values align with your actions, the more authentic you will feel. Others will know where they stand with you, too.

As mentioned, while your values are guides from your past, your identity is your fundamental sense of who you are and is an anchor. We carry strong messages from our past that influence who we believe we are, and they give us a sense of stability. Like values, however, your identity changes over time; this is key to adult development. To achieve your purpose, you may need to examine your sense of identity: you may hold beliefs about yourself that get in your way. Focus on who you need to be to live your purpose.

Values and identity remind us of where we come from – our past and who we are. Sometimes you need to rely on the anchor of identity to feel secure; sometimes you need to reduce the weight of the anchor and explore new territory. Being clear about your past and how it has shaped you, and able to share who you are and what you've learned, is powerful for you and for others.

The two right-hand elements in Figure 2, aspiration and goals, help to bring purpose to life in the future. Aspiration is the big lofty goal, the land in the distance – it's the imagined pinnacle of your life and career. A clear sense of the future, where you are going and why you're going there will propel you forward. Your aspiration is the sense of how you will make your difference in the world. When it's clear, you feel the satisfaction of being on course; it's rewarding to know where you're going and why.

When you've worked on the other three elements, the last step is to turn your intentions into specific actions using short-term goals. Goals are the checkpoints that get you to your aspiration. They make the future tangible. They are what you do today and tomorrow to keep your course true. As you complete your goals, you fuel your motivation – progress feels good, and it motivates further action and further progress, creating a virtuous cycle.

Over the following pages, the elements of the purpose model are discussed in more detail, along with techniques and tools that may help you clarify and define them for yourself. Set aside some time to work through each element. As a generalisation, it makes sense to start with purpose, head to values, then identity, then aspiration, then goals, and finally back to purpose. This is the order used in the rest of this chapter. If you have previously done work on any of the elements, it makes sense to review it: is it up to date or does it need to be refreshed? Another approach is to start with the elements that you are curious about – that you have the most interest in or energy for.

1. Clarify your purpose

Clarifying your purpose is very personal work; do it on your own if you prefer. However, you may find that it's easier to do if you work together with trusted colleagues, family members or friends. On your own, you may get stuck in the detail, or you may miss what's not obvious to you but which stands out to others. Another advantage of working with others is that you'll receive valuable feedback.

A purpose is like a higher-order goal: it's idealistic, enduring and focused on your legacy. What's the difference, or dent, you want to make in your world?

All of us want to make a difference of some kind – what's yours?

To bring your purpose to life, try this activity: imagine yourself at your retirement party. Two or three people step forward to give speeches about you: people who have been important to you in some way during your career. They talk about your achievements, about the person you are, about what role you have played for them and others. In an ideal world, in which you have lived your life with purpose, what would these people say about you?

Simon Sinek suggests that having a purpose is having a 'just cause'.[38] His formula for putting purpose into words is to make it:

1. for something
2. inclusive
3. service oriented
4. resilient
5. idealistic.

What is your just cause?

- What do you care about? Why?
- What are your best skills?
- What matters most to you?
- What is your best possible self?

- How do you want to leave your mark on the world?
- What do the people you admire most do to contribute to the world?

A sentence structure such as the following will help you bring your ideas together succinctly:

I (do something): _____

to (make my difference): _____

so that (there's a better result): _____

Here are some examples of purpose statements:

- 'I help change people for the better, giving them the opportunity to succeed against the odds.'
- 'I promote a stronger awareness of the value of inclusion so that everyone gets to live their full potential.'
- 'I hold myself accountable for leading in a way that leaves people feeling inspired in their work.'

INSIGHT
Purpose helps you live longer

Having a clear purpose in life is not just energising and inspiring, it's also very good for you! Having a purpose in life means that on average you live longer.

Even when controlling for known predictors of longevity, having a purpose in life adds years to it. An increase of one point on a seven-point scale of strength of purpose reduced the risk of dying by 12 per cent, and these results applied regardless of age and working/retirement status.[39] Having a purpose had a unique effect over and above mortality risks and other indicators of psychological and affective wellbeing.

That one-point difference in strength of purpose decreases the risk of heart attack by 27 per cent and stroke by 22 per cent. It slows the progression of Alzheimer's disease. A stronger life purpose has also been associated with a range of other benefits, including more sleep, better sex, less depression and more relaxation.[40] Diabetics are more likely to keep their blood glucose in check. People who begin drug and alcohol rehab with a strong purpose are half as likely to have relapsed six months afterward. Purpose in life is also associated with physiological benefits such as increased levels of natural killer cells that attack viruses and cancers, lower inflammatory cell production, increased 'good' cholesterol and DNA repair.

The good news is, you don't just live longer, you also enjoy your life more!

Can you have too much of a good thing? If it seems like there is too much upside to purpose, here is one caution. If you have *too much* passion for your work, it may *increase* burnout.[41] People who not only love their work but feel that it is an important part of their identity may be unable to let go of it, and from time to time become consumed by it. That usually leads to a sense of conflict between work and life, which is emotionally draining. Burnout may be the result.

However, having a flexAble engagement with work along with a strong sense of purpose means that the conflict is reduced. Engaging in and enjoying activities outside of work replenishes energy, too. There's a positive cycle between purpose experienced in dedication to work and living a rich and meaningful personal life. Purpose lived through work creates a sense of satisfaction, which in turn is a protection against emotional exhaustion.

Marco recognised the potential for burnout in his own sense of purpose. As head of allied health services for a large hospital, he was aware that he and his team shared a passion for their work and were highly dedicated to patient outcomes; that occasionally led to burnout. He also recognised that if he worked on his purpose to integrate it across his work and life, it would be both more meaningful and more workable. He could stay just as passionate and dedicated about his work while doing better at meeting his and his family's needs.

2. Live your values: be authentic

Marco felt out of alignment; his priority value around family wasn't reflected in how he was living his life. The misalignment was uncomfortable for him. Living in line with your values is fundamental for authenticity. Values provide a strong guide to help you navigate the world with confidence and clarity, and meet challenges and setbacks with resilience. They are a compass you can use to stay true to your leadership purpose. Your values guide you, and they provide a guide *to* you, so that others can better understand and connect with you.

What are your core values? Work with values concepts that you already know, or sort and sift through the list of 50 values available on the FlexAbility Resources page on my website (www. karenmorley.com.au/flexability-resources). Identify four to six values of most importance to you, using the following questions:

- What is essential?
- What differentiates you from others?
- Are these values memorable to you and others?
- Do they relate to both character and performance?

Your motivation to lead is also relevant to explore here – how much effort and persistence will you put into pursuing leadership roles and opportunities, into developing as a leader and striving to have a leadership career? Thinking about yourself as a leader may be a strong motivator for you.

Marco identified a set of five values and motivations for himself:

- achievement/success – recognition from others
- family/belonging – connectedness with family
- commitment – energy, consistency, and desire to make a contribution
- flexibility – resilience and adaptability, freedom to make choices to suit his needs
- service – motivation to lead others to achieve valued outcomes.

Values need to be refreshed from time to time. Different life stages and changing responsibilities may signal the need to update to the values that best serve your purpose.

3. Claim your identity: be congruent

Your identity is your unique sense of who you are, and includes your personal qualities, beliefs and personality. Your self-esteem is tied closely to your identity.

To increase your flexAbility as a leader, incorporate it into your identity. Perhaps your focus on accomplishment or success feels like it conflicts with flexAbility; if so, work on how to make them more congruent.

**How does your sense of your identity
serve your purpose and fit with your values?**

A better sense of identity will help you understand patterns of behaviour, habitual conflicts, successes and challenges. To develop a stronger sense of your identity, map its sources. Consider how your identity was formed. What have been your influences? What lessons did you learn from key people or key experiences in your life? How do they shape your sense of who you are?

Consider:

- **your family background** – what key messages do you carry with you from your childhood? Family is our first 'organisation', and parents and caregivers are our first experience of leadership. Where were you in birth order? How was your family structured? How was authority enacted?
- **your social/cultural background** – what key messages do you live out based on important social or cultural patterns to which you have been exposed?
- **professional socialisation** – how was your sense of self and engagement with the world formed through your development as a professional? How important is your work and your professionalism to you? How do leaders in your discipline tend to portray the profession and themselves?
- **your experience of difference** – expectations can be related to your demographic make-up, including gender, culture and race. Your experience of who you are may be shaped by expectations associated with these groups, by conformity with or rejection of them. What groups do you identify with? How does that constrain or enable you?
- **the organisation context** – how have the expectations and cultures of organisations you have worked for shaped your sense of who you are? Your first working experience may have locked in your idea of what a good (or bad) working experience should be and therefore of what kind of leader you want to be, as well as how you see yourself.
- **crucibles and crises** – major events and upheavals in your life – such as moving from one country to another, the loss of significant people in your life or the divorce of your parents – can have a significant impact. What crises have you experienced and what did you learn about yourself in the process?

Reflect on your identity, and articulate the key messages you have learned and how they relate to your sense of identity. Early experience develops the key facets of your identity, then each experience you have in your life confirms or modifies these. The things you pay attention to and do most often have the greatest influence in shaping your identity.

If you want to adapt your identity, ask yourself who it is you seek to be. The other elements in the purpose model will help you to identify what to change to reshape your identity. Your goals will help articulate how to do this.

Try a simple language shift from, for example, 'I want to be more flexible' to 'I am flexAble'. It's by doing things that support your emerging identity that you change it.

4. Imagine your aspiration: be satisfied

Your aspiration is your highest goal for achievement. It provides an orienting point to guide your future focus. It should be satisfying to imagine its achievement, as well as to achieve it.

What would you like to be your biggest achievement? What's your deepest ambition? When you reach the endpoint or pinnacle of your career and life, what would you like to be able to say you have done? What would feel 'worth it'? What would you like your reputation to be?

Here are some example aspirations. You might aspire to be:

- Prime Minister of Australia
- a mentor who helps others achieve their dreams
- leading a small for-purpose organisation
- working in an organisation that has been one of the most significant catalysts for the reduction of human disease in the 21st century

- a millionaire by age 30
- a successful entrepreneur whose services have a global market.

As much as you can, specify the kind of role you would be playing, the accomplishments you would have attained and the industry or organisation you would be working in. You don't have to be as specific as naming the role, such as Prime Minister, unless attaining a particular role is important to you.

Marco's aspiration was to have a senior leadership role with greater autonomy and which allowed him to exercise broader influence in his industry.

5. Achieve your goals: be motivated

Having goals is helpful because they shape the direction of your action, influence the degree of effort you exert and increase your persistence over time. The greater your self-belief, the bigger the goals you can tackle and the better your performance will be.

Setting goals brings about more change, effort, concentration and persistence than merely trying to do your best in the absence of goals. Good intentions are not enough.

Here's what we know about goal-setting:

- **Commitment counts** – high commitment to goals results from believing they are important and attainable. Making goals public demonstrates commitment and increases accountability. The more difficult the goal is, the more commitment is needed.
- **Clarity matters** – articulating goals specifically and clearly identifies the target of change and assists with monitoring and accountability.

- **Feedback helps** – feedback that shows progress increases the likelihood of the goal being achieved and helps maintain momentum.

Using a goal-setting method such as SMART (specific, measurable, achievable, relevant and time-bound) or FAST (frequently discussed, ambitious, specific and transparent) helps to create good goals.

Marco's first goal was to work through the purpose model. He scheduled himself two half-hours over a fortnight to systematically work through each element, reviewing and adjusting his work in the second of those times. He planned to ask his wife and two close colleagues for feedback and advice.

He designed his goals based on doing something flexAble each hour, each day, each week, each month and each quarter. The goals included a daily working hour limit, with a break from 3 to 4 p.m. three days each week to devote to family commitments, a family event each week and an event with extended family each month.

His next step was to plan out his upcoming year and identify milestones that would help him to recalibrate what he did so that he could be more flexAble. His first milestone was to be consistently working five fewer hours per week within three months. His second was a two-part milestone within six months: to be consistently and fluently sharing his purpose statement with others, so that he could strongly agree with the assessment question: 'I have a sense of direction and purpose in life'.

6. Confirm your purpose: be inspired

Working through your values, identity, aspiration and goals helps to clarify your purpose and make it more tangible. Once you have drafted these elements, return to your purpose and adjust it as necessary. Read it aloud; does it make you smile or cringe? If the latter, edit your purpose statement to make it feel real.

When you are clear about what your purpose is, it's easier to direct your efforts in line with it.

Public health and wellbeing expert Victor Strecher points out that to keep focused on your purpose requires energy – yet, at the same time, clarity of purpose is a source of energy.[42] Feeling a sense of agency, that you are aligned with your purpose, generates energy.

If you're not yet as clear about your purpose as you would like to be, try the following:

- Read more about purpose (for example, read biographies of people whose achievements were based on their purpose) or find out more about your role models and identify what their purpose is.
- Identify what annoys or particularly aggravates you – what if you could change that?
- Think about the kind of future you want for your children or other young people; what do you want the world to be like for them? How do/might you contribute to that world?
- Think about your own advantages. If you are able to 'count your blessings', you are more likely to try to contribute to making a better world. What might you be motivated to 'give back'?

Ask for suggestions from people who know you well. What would they imagine your purpose is or could be?

Keep working at it: it will get easier!

Finally, give your purpose the 'heart and soul test': if you achieved your purpose, would it feel like all your dreams had come true?

RESET YOUR PURPOSE

Purpose is energising. When your energy is directed towards your purpose, engagement and performance will increase. Having a sense of purpose helps you take setbacks and failures in your stride and provides you with the ongoing capacity to generate new possibilities. It increases your resilience.

To recap – use these six steps to reset your purpose. It's key to increasing your flexAbility.

1. Clarify your purpose. What do you stand for? What is your cause?

2. Live your values. What values make you feel your most authentic?

3. Claim your identity. Know who you really are and why flexAbility works for you.

4. Imagine your aspiration. Orient yourself towards your highest ambition, your pinnacle achievement.

5. Set your goals to get motivated. What do you need to do to live a life filled with purpose?

6. Confirm your purpose. Give it the 'heart and soul' test and be inspired.

CHAPTER 3

BE PSYCHOLOGICALLY FLEXIBLE

'Between stimulus and response there is a space.
In that space is our power to choose our response.
In our response lies our growth and freedom.'
– Attributed to Victor Frankl[43]

Marlena is a senior operational manager who often leads high-profile cross-functional projects. She's considered to have high potential – yet there are questions about her appetite for promotion. She has the capability to be successful at more senior levels, but does she want to take that next step?

Marlena hesitated to say yes to more senior roles because she felt that it was a massive challenge just to do her existing role well. She had created a successful approach to her work, flexibly managing her time and priorities; she knew how to keep the plates spinning. She was concerned that maintaining her fine balance would not be possible with additional responsibilities.

She wanted to make her work and life goals compatible, rather than competitive, so that she could advance as she desired without sacrificing her life, relationships and wellbeing to do it.

Just after Marlena made the decision that she would pursue advancement, a workload crunch upset her fine balance, which threatened her new resolve. If she couldn't manage the workload expectations at this level, how could she take on more responsibility?

In this chapter, I'll share how working on her thinking, feeling and learning made an enormous difference to Marlena's ability to navigate her circumstances. FlexAbility means being psychologically flexible; it means being able to make choices about your thinking and feeling, and to always be learning. By thinking mindfully, Marlena was able to fine-tune how she made sense of what happened around her. By freeing her feelings, she was less caught up in unpleasant emotions. By learning openly, she was able to focus on how to make progress aligned with her purpose.

Assess your psychological flexibility

Marlena's psychological flexibility needs recalibration. How is yours?

1. How easily do you shift your thinking to make sure you are focused on what's most important to you?

2. How free are you of feelings like self-doubt, failing, shame, fear and anger?

3. How readily do you absorb new information and seek learning?

4. How satisfied are you that your thinking, feeling and learning serve your purpose and values?

5. Which area would you most like to work on – thinking, feeling or learning?

To regain her balance, Marlena needed more flexibility in her thinking, feeling and learning, as represented in Figure 3. It starts with thinking mindfully. That means being able to observe what is happening to your thinking, to have different ways to understand what is going on. How we make sense of things affects how we feel about them.

Sometimes we are caught up in unhelpful thinking, like a deer in the headlights. Marlena found herself stuck in the mind-trap of accepting all work requests to prove that she was worthy of her job. She felt she 'couldn't say no' to anything, because that would mean she 'couldn't make flexibility work'. A reality check on that suggested that she accepted more work than her peers and set a higher standard for it. She was *over-proving* her ability to meet demands.

Saying no *had* to be an option. Yet to prove that she could meet demands, she kept accepting work long past the point of reasonableness. She couldn't think of anything to delegate; only she could do the work. That set her up to feel badly about herself. She was afraid of asking for help from her boss or her team. Her biggest fear was that she would be seen as incapable of doing her job well, and she was unable to recognise that she was the only person who might do that.

Her deftly spinning plates were now whirling wildly and about to crash to the ground. Her brain felt 'fragmented', her self-talk had become negative and punitive. Stuck thoughts and feelings fed on each other in a negative spiral; she needed to elevate, to rise above any one way of seeing things, to avoid that.

She was hooked! Her thoughts were inflexible, her feelings were stuck. She'd lost her ability to identify possibilities and alternatives. She couldn't see her way out. She was close to burning out.

Learning takes curiosity, and curiosity used intentionally helps to fine-tune feelings. If Marlena can see subtleties and nuances, she can express her feelings in a more refined way and can hold them more lightly. Learning openly also means that you extend your thinking, identifying new perspectives that free you up and make room for choice.

Figure 3: Three elements of psychological flexibility

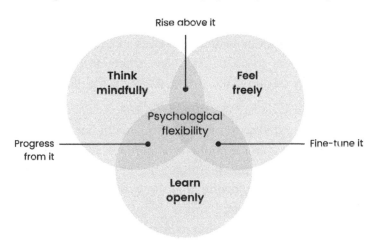

Think mindfully: manage your attention

At the heart of how we respond to situations is what sense we make of them. That impacts our emotions and the choices we make.

Attention is perhaps the most precious of resources for leaders, given the significant demands they face. The more mindful you are, and the better you manage your thoughts, the less likely you are to be captured by unhelpful thinking. When you are mindful, you actively manage your attention.

It's all too easy to think rigidly. We tend to avoid facing mental challenges and instead disappear into worry, distraction and rumination. A part of Marlena's mental challenge, for example, was to stop believing she was unworthy if she didn't accept every work request. She'd begun toying with the idea of giving up her career dreams to avoid these feelings and was starting to create a storyline to justify it to herself.

We are always trying to make sense and meaning out of what is going on around us. Mindfulness helps us to notice our thoughts without being consumed by them. That creates a distance (the space that Frankl writes of in the quotation at the start of this chapter) that allows us to free ourselves of thoughts that aren't helpful. It allows us to notice those thoughts, consider how well they serve us and make choices to work with them or to let them go.

Marlena needed to discover how to think about her situation in a more workable way. If she could think about what was happening with greater mindfulness, she might not be trapped by it. Being more mindful, and knowing that how she thinks about her situation has an impact on its workability, will help her to create greater congruence between her aspiration and her reality.

Being mindful about our thinking means accepting reality for what it is, without denying it or feeling stuck in it. We're not fused with the current reality or one 'right way'. We are open to possibility, to alternative ways of thinking.

Mindful thinking means being present in the moment with full awareness and openness.

Mindfulness is a fundamental practice for managing your attention and creating calm. Marlena's starting point was to establish a regular mindfulness practice that involved focusing on her breath and her present sensations. She committed to 15 minutes of daily practice, scheduling it into her diary just after lunch, and over time this increased her sense of ease.

Another excellent mindfulness practice is the STOP technique, which is outlined later in this book, on page 91. Further information is available from the Center for Mindfulness at the University of California San Diego: it has a series of practices that can be downloaded on SoundCloud, as well as other resources on mindfulness (https://cih.ucsd.edu/mindfulness/guided-audio-video).

Then Marlena focused on the things that mattered the most, keeping it basic and aligned with purpose. That meant looking after herself, spending time with family and taking breaks to recharge. This helped to relieve some of the pressure she was feeling. The idea was to narrow the complexity of her current experience, to shift her perspective, as her first step.

Feel freely: increase your emotional agility

Rowan was responsible for his organisation's crisis response to the pandemic – and he found himself stuck fixing daily crises. While, in a sense, it was why the role existed, he often felt frustrated by having to focus on minor problems.

Rowan's thinking led to some unhelpful feelings. He thought a couple of members of the crisis-response team weren't systematic in their thinking, and that the crisis-focus was feeding their sense of self-importance. He felt responsible for making sure things were done 'the right way'. He felt let down by his colleagues. He was disappointed and frustrated.

So, he sought to get a better perspective on the situation. He needed something more workable: a perspective that created rather than reduced options for everyone.

Viewing the same situation from multiple positions helped Rowan to increase his flexAbility. When he shifted out of first person – 'I', 'me' and 'my' – and into third person – 'we' – he was able to plot his interactions with his colleagues to notice the patterns.

He shifted into second person to imagine the perspectives of his 'problem' colleagues. He humanised them by thinking about their needs and interests, and what he knew about their personal circumstances. His empathy for their experiences immediately increased his compassion. They stopped being 'the problem'.

Seeing the situation from different perspectives changed how Rowan felt. 'Feeling freely' is the ability to create space between the event and your feelings. In that space, which only needs to be seconds, you have the chance to question your immediate response, to check its value and to identify what emotional need guides your response. You can take different perspectives, which creates new options.

It isn't that we shouldn't have feelings that aren't pleasant; the challenge is how to live calmly with them. Not to get rid of them, but to make them workable. It is what we do when we feel 'bad' that matters. We need to accept that our fundamental human condition involves unpleasant feelings.[44] We are not flawed because we get angry, depressed or hurt – we get angry, depressed or hurt because we're human.

How well do your feelings serve you and your intentions? You get to decide how helpful a feeling is, and to let it go or to work with it.[45]

Rowan's ability to recognise his feelings, to pause and explore their value to him, made an enormous difference to his energy and his self-management. Noticing his emotional responses and needs meant that he could work out the best way to meet them. He felt responsible, frustrated and hurt because he cared, and recognising this meant that he could choose different ways to experience caring and to show his care.

By making space between stimulus and response, we get the time to reflect on our purpose and values. We have a chance to be our better selves, and to act in a way that serves us best. In that space, we can shift from reacting to experiences to choosing responses that allow us to pursue our purpose.

Rowan paused to consider what his colleagues' emotional needs might be. He chose to ask them about their needs, rather than believe that he knew what they were. That stopped him from feeling that he was at their whim and from taking their actions personally. They weren't about him at all!

Name your feelings

There are so many words for different emotions, yet we tend to use few of them. The more words for emotions you use, however, the freer your feelings become.

According to adult developmental coach and author Jennifer Garvey Berger, 'people who name emotional nuance are better able to recover from setbacks, can better manage their anxiety and sadness, and generally cope better with the unexpected difficulties of life'.[46]

If you want to increase your emotions vocabulary, try using the Wheel of Emotions chart, which is available on the FlexAbility Resources page of my website (www.karenmorley.com.au/flexability-resources). Try to be much more specific about what your feeling is: start at the centre of the Wheel and work your way outward to find the word that best fits what you're feeling. Gamify it – see how many emotion words you can use in a day or a week. Share the Wheel with your friends, family and colleagues and see who has the biggest vocab.

Learn openly: be contagiously curious

In one sense, we are never not learning. Our fast, automatic brains are always busy in the background, creating associations and learning. That might seem like a benefit – it's happening without effort – but it can also work against us. If our conscious, executive brain isn't overseeing what we're learning, the learning may not align with our values and intentions. This is how we can become biased without realising it.

A conscious learning stance may be a little slower, but it will be aligned with your purpose and values.

Priming learning by priming curiosity is a great way to get the balance right. Staying curious, promoting an appetite for exploration and discovery, is the engine room of learning. It supports both thinking mindfully and feeling freely. Curiosity means exploring, seeking out, immersing yourself to discover what's new. Being curious means stepping into uncertainty as something to explore, rather than something to fear or avoid.

As distinguished psychology professor and author Todd Kashdan and positive psychologist Robert Biswas-Diener say, 'curiosity is not a fixed characteristic. It's a strength we can develop and wield on the path to a more fulfilling life'.[47]

INSIGHT
Curiosity primes learning and is rewarding too

The great advantage of curiosity is that when we pursue the new and spend time engaging with it, we increase the shape, size and number of neurons in our brain and the connections between them. That helps us to become more efficient in making decisions about the future.[48]

The value of priming curiosity is twofold. First, it helps create new options and new knowledge. Yet there's an even greater value. The emotional state of curiosity is highly rewarding in and of itself. When we are motivated, curious, in control or mindful, the brain generates a burst of dopamine. This is the reward neurotransmitter, and it facilitates learning. It produces a good mood and provides positive reinforcement.

When we're curious and exploring the world, we get both the excitement of seeking new rewards and the fulfilment of experiencing them. More dopamine is produced when we are attracted to something that evokes curiosity and interest – something that stretches us to our learning edge. When what we are doing is meaningful and important to us (for example, because it relates to important people in our lives), there is even greater brain activity and a bigger dopamine burst.

If our curious exploration and engagement is positive, we also experience a surge of endorphins. As the body's natural opiates, these give us a mood boost. If we feel tension and frustration when learning, however, we only get the benefit of dopamine, not endorphins.

By contrast, if we feel anxious rather than curious when we experience uncertainty, it evokes a stress response. Cortisol is released, and this interferes with concentration. We'll most likely want to relieve the tension and so will stop being curious. Prolonged stress interferes with the ability to learn: it negatively impacts wellbeing by causing social pain and increasing negative thoughts.

Curiosity mitigates the stress that arises from engaging with new, complex, uncertain or unfamiliar experiences.

There's plenty of potential benefit in being curious and giving up certainty. Find the time for more curiosity. While many leaders are time-poor because of overwork demands, a good deal of time is being wasted, in that the amount of time people spend dealing with unimportant tasks is increasing. Josh Bersin, Founder and President of talent management firm Bersin & Associates, reports that in one study, 27 per cent of 2400 professionals felt that they were wasting a staggering 20 per cent or more of their time on email that wasn't relevant to their work.[49]

The study also found that there is a huge benefit from increasing the amount of learning that you do. 'Heavy' learners, who engage in more than five hours of learning per week, have significantly better outcomes than those who are 'light' learners, engaging in learning for less than one hour per week. In Bersin's research, heavy learners were half as stressed, 23 per cent more likely to take on extra responsibility, much more likely to find purpose in their work and 39 per cent more likely to feel productive and successful.

People who spend a lot of their time learning enjoy their work more and are more confident, productive, happy and successful.

While many leaders struggle to fit learning into a crammed work schedule, doing so yields significant benefits. Reclaiming that 20 per cent of time wasted on unimportant tasks to use for learning seems worth it!

Asking open-ended questions is a helpful tactic for learning. These questions start with 'what', 'how', 'when', 'who' and 'why'. Try these question starters to help get you into a state of curiosity:

- What if...?
- How else...?
- I wonder...?
- Why not... (do the opposite to...)?
- What would happen if we didn't...?

And try these questions:

- What don't I know about this situation/person? What might I learn from this situation/person?
- What do I believe? How might my thinking be wrong/limited?
- What's another way to think about this? And yet another? And still another?
- How does our disagreement help us to increase the possibilities?
- What can I enable?

These questions help shift your perspective, which helps you to be more flexAble; they're an absolute must for a world made more complex and in which there are no easy answers. The more mindful you are in your thinking, the less stuck you feel. Being less 'fused' to any one way of doing things opens you to multiple alternatives for the future, which sparks a sense of hope.

Increase your learning to increase your resilience against unhelpful thinking and feeling. It will then become easier to see connections between ideas, and to be more creative.

RESET YOUR PSYCHOLOGICAL FLEXIBILITY

If you work on your psychological flexibility, you can balance your future focus with day-to-day realities. You'll be able to pay attention to what matters most, regulate your feelings, reduce burnout and feel aligned with your purpose.

In summary, use the four-step process we've discussed in this chapter to reset your thinking, feeling and learning:

1. Be mindful. Notice how you make sense of what's happening. Do you need a fresh perspective?

2. Allow yourself to feel whatever it is you are feeling. Do your feelings serve your purpose?

3. Be curious. Get intentional. What can you learn from the situation you are in?

4. Remind yourself of your purpose and values. What thinking, feeling and learning serves you best?

PART II

Do what matters

*'People who try to push too many goals at once
usually wind up doing a mediocre job on all of them.
You can ignore the principle of focus,
but it won't ignore you.'*

CHRIS McCHESNEY et al.[50]

WHEN YOU know what matters, it's so much easier to do what matters. If you're a high achiever, work is a source of pride and the pursuit of success is in your DNA – but there are limits. It's critical to know where yours are and how you can maintain the balance that helps you perform at a high level without burning out.

Who wouldn't want to work fewer hours, get more done and love your work even more than you already do? This second part of the book shows you how to do this.

Chapter 4 starts with the premise that loving your work is a good thing, and that structure is the way to achieve it. A work structure that emphasises organising, prioritising and digitising will reduce 'system noise'. Organise your job so that you play to your strengths. Prioritise your work to make it easy to do what's most important. Use technology to make work tasks easier and to create better connections with others.

In the busy fray of the usual working day, it can be hard to find the time to focus on meaningful work. It's a common issue: the most important work and the most difficult decisions don't get enough time. It takes dedicated focus, and busyness is the archenemy of focus. Chapter 5 outlines a process for managing your attention, keeping yourself aligned with your purpose and doing deep, focused work.

Then, to make everything easier, Chapter 6 focuses on how to identify and replace unhelpful habits with newer, better ones. Habits help your hard work to stick. When what's most important to you is embedded in habits, it becomes effortless: producing high-quality output becomes routine.

Adjust these three levers – structure, focus and habits – to make it easier to do what matters most.

CHAPTER 4

LOVE YOUR WORK STRUCTURE

'*[H]aving control over when, where and how you work matters a great deal. It signals trust and reliability... when people have the opportunity to work virtually and the flexibility to arrange the job tasks there is an increase in commitment, performance and retention.*' – Tsedal Neeley[51]

Dev found that he was constantly caught up in the day-to-day and didn't spend enough time focused on strategic priorities. Organising and prioritising took time and required concentration and a different thinking pattern, so he tended to put it off until he was able to devote the right kind of attention to it.

Dev realised the irony of this: by continuing to put off his work on strategic priorities, he was unable to get on top of them. He wasn't spending enough time on the work that was both most important for the job and most satisfying to do.

Then the pandemic hit. For months, he and his team scrambled to deal with new technology rollouts, adjusting work processes and meeting new demands. The disarray he'd felt before the pandemic began to escalate out of control.

Dev sought a fresh way to structure his and his teams' work to get them off the back foot. He'd recruited well, and his team had so much potential, but they weren't leveraging it. He wanted to love, not endure, his work.

In this chapter, the focus is on how to increase the enjoyment you get from your work. Overworking and too many demands can take some of the pleasure out of work. Having a clear purpose and a firm resolve to avoid burnout won't automatically make relentless everyday pressures and demands disappear.

What you need are some everyday practices to minimise and manage the demands. To maintain your enjoyment and the love you have for your work, use a strong work structure that has three elements:

1. organising – organise your work to maximise your best skills and abilities

2. prioritising – prioritise your work so that you achieve what's most important

3. digitising – digitise processes to support what you are trying to achieve.

This chapter will help you to review your existing structure and highlight how you can improve it.

Assess your work structure

How well does your current work structure serve you and your purpose? Use this assessment to identify where you can improve:

1. How often do you feel like you are working at your best, making the most of your strengths and passions?

2. How often do you feel like you are caught up in a whirlwind, with too many things to do and not enough time to do them well?

3. To what extent does technology make your work easier?

4. What are your biggest obstacles to loving your work?

5. What areas do you need to focus on to increase your love for your work?

The 'organise, prioritise, digitise' sequence, which is highlighted in Figure 4 (overleaf), will help give you the structure needed to do what you love:

- The first step is to align your work with your purpose by job crafting so that your strengths, motivations and passions shine. Organise your work responsibilities so that you can perform at your best, and help others do the same.

- Second, prioritise your work. Don't let the whirlwind of 'too much to do and not enough time to do it in' overwhelm you. Keep your priorities clear and at the front and centre of your attention. The 'four disciplines' method outlined later in this chapter will help here.

- Third, digitise. The sudden shift to remote work in 2020 meant we had to rely on digital as never before. There was a lot of learning in that, and we've made a few mistakes along the way – one of which was to let digital be the priority. Instead, structure your use of your digital tools to enable, rather than undermine, getting the important work done.

Figure 4: Organise, prioritise, then digitise

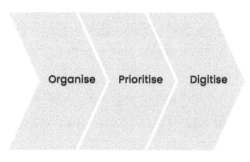

Let's explore this process in more detail.

Organise

'Job crafting' is a technique created by Amy Wrzesniewski and colleagues[52] which enables you to proactively organise the work you do. The technique helps you to align your strengths, motivations and passions to your work requirements to make work more meaningful and enjoyable. As leader, help your team members to craft their jobs so that they too find greater meaning and enjoyment. According to Wrzesniewski, people who 'craft' their job perform significantly better than those who don't.

Job crafting means you shape your work in line with what you are required to do, as well as what you are good at, what motivates and drives you. You don't have carte blanche to do work that's not relevant or to avoid your job accountabilities. The critical thing job crafting does is to give a sense of control and agency. As we saw in Chapter 1, autonomy in your work helps to prevent burnout.

**Job crafting prompts you to visualise your job,
map its elements and then reorganise them
to better suit you.**

Job crafting focuses on three core aspects of work. The first is work tasks. The process starts with mapping the tasks you spend your time on and assessing their fit. To get a better fit, you might change the boundaries of your job by adding or deleting tasks. Alternatively, you might adjust the scope of some tasks by expanding or diminishing them. You might also change the way that you do the tasks.

The second core aspect of work that can be crafted is relationships. You can change the nature or extent of your interactions with others. For example, one thing that Dev aspired to do was to mentor junior team members. He never seemed to be able to find the time to mentor them, so he used job crafting to prioritise more time for this.

Changing perceptions is the third aspect of job crafting. You might reframe your whole job: what's its purpose? Or you could think about the purpose of some aspects of your job. Dev, for instance, found the day-to-day problem-solving he was doing unrewarding, and while he needed to reduce how much of this he did, he couldn't stop doing it altogether. So, he reframed it as a small task, contrasting it with the more important, strategic part of his work.

INSIGHT

Job satisfaction increases self-efficacy, hope, resilience and optimism

How does job crafting work? It has a positive influence on 'psychological capital', which in turn positively affects both job satisfaction and career success, measured as promotions over time.[53]

Psychological capital is defined as a combination of self-efficacy, optimism, resilience and hope:

- **Self-efficacy** – the confidence to take on and succeed at challenging tasks

- **Optimism** – the positive expectation that you will succeed

- **Resilience** – the ability to bounce back and succeed when faced with problems or setbacks

- **Hope** – the degree of perseverance in pursuing goals and redirecting actions to succeed.[54]

The key influence of job crafting is via personal agency. People creatively adapt their job to their needs, goals and preferences, and that impacts on their perception of job demands and job resources. Overall, they achieve their personal goals and adjust their work to get a better person–job fit.

People with lower levels of psychological capital tend to avoid anything that may lead to loss of resources, and are thus less likely to engage in job crafting. Those with higher levels are likely to do so independently. To assist your team members, whatever their level of psychological capital, help them to understand what to do to craft their job and how to do it. Provide them with positive feedback, encouragement and support to increase their self-efficacy. Increase their optimism by giving them increased control over their work.

Also ensure that the initiatives they undertake are realistic. Give them a reasonable level of autonomy to adapt their job tasks in line with their preferences.

Craft your work

To craft his job, Dev looked at it as a series of building blocks. The first step was to be very clear about what the building blocks were and how much time he spent on each. Larger blocks represented the tasks that took the most time, and smaller blocks were the tasks that took the least time. His map confirmed the imbalance he felt in how he was spending his time. He spent most of his time firefighting, dealing with day-to-day problems. He devoted the least amount of time to strategy, culture and supporting his team members. While Dev already knew that this was the case, mapping it out in this way reinforced his resolve to make change.

To identify how best to change how he spent his time, Dev first identified his motives, strengths and passions. These are the three important considerations which determine whether a job is engaging and inspiring. He was motivated by working strategically, building a positive team culture and supporting his team members so that they could do their best work. Dev's strengths were strategic thinking, influencing senior stakeholders, leadership coaching and commercial acumen. His three top passions were creating business impact, supporting others' growth and development, and seeing others flourish.

Dev then created a revised set of task blocks whose sizes better indicated how he wanted to spend his time, energy and attention. He drew rectangles around groups of tasks which were similar, ending up with four task groups. These helped to frame his job, and he described these as four clear roles that he needed to play to be successful.

The new task groups were: implementing strategic priorities, managing stakeholders, empowering his teams to be high performing, and creating connections and synergies within the branch.

The final step in this job crafting exercise was to turn the new job configuration into a reality. For Dev that was relatively easy. His job crafting was helpful in recasting the time that he needed to allocate to tasks and relationships.

Dev introduced job crafting to his team, as he appreciated that having a sense of control and autonomy over work was inspiring and empowering for everyone. He shared with his teams what he'd done and how he'd done it. He began guiding his managers to craft their own roles and encouraged them to cascade the process through the branch. Some team members focused on relationships, emphasising those that energised them. Some focused on their own perceptions of the work that they were doing to reframe it. Others identified ways to grow their jobs.

Collaborating to identify better ways of distributing tasks meant that they could craft their work to be more inspiring to each of them. Joe took on the management of several processes from two of his colleagues. He enjoyed and was good at process management, much more so than they were. Joe was able to introduce several innovations into process management, which were then rolled out to other teams. Meanwhile, Joe's colleagues, freed up from process management, spent more time with their stakeholders, increasing their influence and enjoyment.

It's important that people understand the boundaries around job crafting, however. It's not a licence to take over other people's work or to stop doing the work that's expected of you. Equally, while job crafting allows people to challenge themselves, it's important not to get too excited and take on too much. Changes in job design should always be discussed with the team and manager.

To be successful, job crafting needs to focus on creating value for others, building trust and identifying people who will work with you.

Aligning your work tasks with these fundamentals gives you an opportunity to renew your clarity about your work and feel greater ease amid the challenges. Don't let yourself be too limited by job descriptions, demands from above or what anyone else says you should be doing. We're all facing some tough stuff right now, but that doesn't mean that you shouldn't or can't love your work. It's even more important that you do.

Stop the meeting madness

The second key aspect of organising work is to set an appropriate cadence for meetings, with clear agendas and frequencies. Meetings are one of the most common methods we use to get work done, yet they are one of the biggest time sinks of the working day. Question the purpose, focus and duration of all meetings to ensure that they contribute the right value. According to meeting consultant and researcher Steven G. Rogelberg, about 50 per cent of meeting time is considered ineffective,[55] so there's a lot of opportunity for improvement.

Imagine a schedule of meetings that creates positive and energising outcomes, improves your decision-making, increases team cohesion and motivation and saves you time! How much more you could love your work! It is possible, but only if you get rigorous about your meeting cadence.

Rather than accept that time confetti is an inevitable consequence of a busy 21st century working world, see yourself as a time steward. Leadership is a service to others, including to their time. Time is a precious resource, not something to fritter away like confetti. Be intentional about making smart meeting choices so that people love attending them and get quality work done.

Many leaders tend to be caught in the grip of a continuous stream of meetings, leaving little time for thinking and reflection. Remote meetings via videoconference seem to exacerbate this. This was part of Dev's problem: 12 hours of back-to-back videoconference meetings daily were taking a heavy toll.

Meetings are fine when they have a clear function, purpose and agenda, and are facilitated well. But when they're continuous, it's almost impossible for them to be productive. There is simply not enough time to prepare, or to follow up. When they are poorly run, they waste not just time but emotional energy, as people need to recover from them![56]

Establish a routine of meetings that help get good work done. Help yourself and your team to manage your time and outputs well and stay connected to, and engaged with, each other. Here's how:

1. Reduce the number of meetings you have and make them decision-based; share information in other ways.

2. Always give yourself a time buffer between meetings: don't schedule them back-to-back.

3. Reduce meeting times – make them 15 minutes or 25 minutes, not 30 minutes. That helps with breaks. It also helps with focus; when there is a degree of time pressure, we increase our focus and engagement, which improves meeting performance.

4. Prepare well. Engage people in creating the agenda – always have a clear, action-oriented agenda – and confirm it, clarifying the decisions that need to be made. People then have a clear goal and intent to guide their participation.

5. Invite only those people required to make the decision.

6. Begin with the most important items.

7. Use inclusive practices such as taking turns and inviting contributions to give and get full value from each person.

8. If the meeting is remote, record it so that others can review it. They can save time by reviewing at double speed.

9. Make meeting endings explicit. Confirm the agenda that has been covered and the actions that have been agreed. If you finish early, reward everyone by allowing a recharge break.

10. Always follow up on outcomes and responsibilities in due course.

One further note regarding point 3, meeting times – while reducing the length of meetings is generally helpful, the reverse may be true for some meetings. You may need to make some longer to allow time for deliberation, creativity and debate. Making sure the meeting length is fit for purpose is what matters.

Stop exhausting your conscious mind by careening from one meeting to the next, making lots of minor decisions that often don't work out or get follow-through. Save your brainpower for where it really counts, where it would do most value and where you would feel most satisfaction.

These are the meetings that matter most

Many leaders get trapped in a cycle of problem-solving meetings. Instead, establish a structured cadence of meetings, such as these listed here, to proactively manage your team's shared work.

- **One-to-one check-ins with each team member** – focus on personal connection and building relationships. In these meetings, you are in service to your team member. What's on their mind? What's working well? How are they dealing with their latest challenge? What help can you provide them? What do they need more information about? What progress are they making? These meetings should happen weekly.

- **Team check-ins** – focus on progress. These should happen roughly fortnightly and focus on shared work goals and problems.

- **Monthly check-ins** – focus on cohesion. They allow time to attend to team norms, dynamics and cohesion, and to surface shared issues.
- **Alignment check-ins** – focus on direction and purpose. These need to occur between monthly and quarterly, depending on how well your team works together and how much remote work you are doing. They help to celebrate progress, provide news about major updates and engage with senior leaders on organisational priorities. These sessions allow the team to work on the team, to renew psychological safety and trust, engage newer team members, recalibrate major team processes, call out and resolve conflict and increase collaboration.
- **(Bi)annual check-ins** – focus on strategy review and reset. These should be longer meetings held every six to twelve months, providing a focused opportunity to review and reset strategy. These meetings take more planning and create more significant follow-up actions.

> **Organise your meetings around a focused structure and cadence to increase their value. This sets you up well to both identify and then deliver on priority work.**

Prioritise

Once you've organised work tasks and meetings, structure in a strong prioritisation regime.

Most organisations have sufficient strategic focus; what they lack is execution focus. Ensuring alignment between the highest-level outcomes and what individuals do day-to-day is challenging. It's not simply a matter of knowing what needs to be done but of being prepared to do it. I recommend the Four Disciplines of Execution approach: combined with a regular cadence of the meetings identified in the previous section, it will lead to increased understanding, acceptance and accountability.

Bring a new discipline to your work

The Four Disciplines of Execution[57] help to translate strategies and job descriptions into specific work tasks. This is a simple yet effective method that creates a deeper, clearer focus on the work that has highest priority. Niko, Managing Director of an operations-based organisation, used it successfully to create a shared focus for her team on its most important work.

The four disciplines are as follows:

1. **Focus on the wildly important** – we're generally caught up in a whirlwind of trying to do too much, and that makes it harder to get anything done. Focusing on a few things that are most important creates a clearer message to the team and simplifies effort. Ask yourself, what's the one thing that is most important right now?

2. **Act on lead measures** – usually we focus on lag measures, but the problem with them is that we get the data on performance once it's over. Lead measures turn that around and help you focus on behaviours that you have direct control over. Customer satisfaction is a lag indicator, whereas improved customer relationship management is a lead indicator. Number of injuries is a lag measure, whereas percentage of people wearing hard hats is a lead measure. Lead measures are predictive, and using them helps you to see what will impact your work in the future. They have a positive impact on goal achievement.

3. **Keep a compelling scoreboard** – keep a scorecard of your lead measures; make it something that everyone has easy access to, and tick off your progress. For example, if you

want your team leaders to develop specific skills in their team members, your lead indicator might be time spent coaching. Your target might be four hours a week. Your team leaders can tick this off the scorecard as it's done. The scorecard could also show when a new skill is learned. That way you can see both the tangible results and how much coaching is required to achieve them.

4. **Create a cadence of accountability** – put in place a cadence of regular and frequent meetings for those who own the goals. Use these to help everyone check off their actions on the scorecard. This will make it immediately obvious when things are on and off track and make it possible to take early action to remedy problems.

You can't focus on everything: use the Four Disciplines with your team to do what's most important right now.

Niko found that the Four Disciplines approach had an enormous impact on how she saw her role in getting work done and generated a great deal of excitement in her team. She had felt that the business was beset by problems that weren't being solved without her direct attention. They were behind in their revenue targets. She was two years into her stint as Managing Director and felt that there should have been more progress. She couldn't seem to elevate the team's concerns to match her own.

Niko introduced the Four Disciplines to the team using the whirlwind metaphor (see point 1 in the previous list), and it resonated with them. As she introduced the disciplines and told the team that she wanted them to take ownership, they became animated and engaged. As she put it, she couldn't have been happier with their response.

They'd been unclear about their focus, and their reliance on lag indicators hadn't been providing insight into their problems. Niko had been taking too much control and responsibility for the solutions. 'It feels like I have a new team', she said. 'The relief that I feel is amazing.'

Digitise

The third part of structuring work is to consider how digital tools can help you get work done. Once work roles and tasks are clear and prioritised, the right tools can be mobilised. Technology offers so many options that support quality work practices and make collaboration easier – useful when people are in the same office, but critical when they work across multiple sites.

Remote work isn't new, it's been around for some time, but it took the pandemic to see widespread uptake outside the tech industry. Since the beginning of the pandemic, the necessity to quickly introduce digital tools has been a major challenge.[58] Many organisations grapple with return-to-office policies – with some aiming for 100 per cent return – while others have abandoned the office altogether. Most organisations are not at either of these extremes, of course, but a key aspect of this struggle is how digital tools support work wherever it is done.

Tsedal Neeley, in her book *Remote Work Revolution: Succeeding from Anywhere,* reinforces the benefits of remote work: increases in productivity, decreases in commute times and operating costs, and access to a broader talent pool.

But there are plenty of wrinkles too. It's easier to get into what Neeley calls 'out-of-sight, out-of-sync, out-of-touch' mode, and to blur the boundaries between work and non-work. Despite that, 87 per cent of people say they prefer to work at least partly remotely.[59]

Remote or hybrid work arrangements are best when they:

- consider employees' needs (which aren't all the same) and also organisational needs (which vary over time)
- start with the work that needs to be done, and then address how best to get it done
- pay attention to belonging and engagement.

Neeley claims that teams are always worse off if they don't have a proper launch session.

'Launching' a remote team is critical. The purpose of a launch meeting is to ensure that everyone understands and agrees on how to work together.

There are four elements that need to be covered and agreed upon at a launch session:

1. clear and simple goals for the team
2. each person's role, functions and constraints
3. the resources that are available
4. norms for collaborating.

For remote teams, there should be relaunches every six to eight weeks to reinforce psychological safety and update norms and communication.

Team members need a chance to offer input, ask questions, pose concerns and get updates on changes. The overall purpose is alignment. People need to know where they fit in the team. They need to understand everyone else's roles. They need to be able to discuss and resolve competing commitments and different expectations.

Like all good meetings, remote meetings rely on good preparation. Team and meeting norms are fundamental. They create mutual expectations about what makes a good remote meeting – for example, 'Let's keep all responses to no more than 60 seconds so that everyone has a chance to speak'. Especially for longer meetings, schedule breaks and take them on time. Encourage people to stretch and move. Actively facilitate the meeting. Rather than asking questions like 'Are there any comments?', call on each person to comment in turn. Politely interrupt and move people along to manage time well. Use polls, chat and other tools to increase involvement, as well.

Team norms include helping to keep the distinction between work and home as clear as possible, and that's especially difficult if people are working across multiple time zones. Consider limiting correspondence to agreed business hours, and confirm expectations for punctuality and attendance. Ask people what will help them to manage the boundary between work and home.

It's also important to acknowledge the potential for isolation.[60] If you show strong commitment in these four areas, no matter where your team members live, they will feel less isolated, more motivated and better invested in the team.

Be productive remotely

There need be no drop in productivity when you work remotely – but the right tools need to be used in the right ways. With the pivot to remote work, some organisations have introduced digital surveillance tools to track productivity. Don't use these tools. They signal mistrust, and that undermines motivation and team commitment.

Teams that have strong relationships, perhaps extending to friendships outside of the office, don't need to use richer technology such as video conferencing as frequently. They already know each other and have multiple connection points, so 'leaner' tools, such as email and shared documents, may suffice more often for them.

However, where teams have neutral relationships – for example, they are brought together randomly – richer forms of communication work well.

Somewhat counter-intuitively, teams that have a history of disagreement or antagonism are worse at negotiating and making decisions when they use richer technologies. So, pay attention to relationships and team norms with teams that don't work well together. Use shared folders and social and collaboration tools while you improve working relationships. As the team dynamics improve, you can increase the use of richer technology tools and facilitate interactions tightly.

We've tended to over-rely on video conferencing tools. Anita Woolley and her colleagues say that audio-conferencing calls increase collective intelligence, so don't discount their value as an important collaboration tool. People are more likely to take turns and have equal speaking time on audio calls.[61] Task-focused conversations are better over audio, so that people can also review relevant documents.

Human interaction is 'bursty', alternating between collaboration and individual work. Take this into account as you plan your work. Aim for multiple communication methods and mix between them to manage fatigue and get the best work outcomes.

It might seem counter-intuitive, but redundant communication helps to cut through overload.

Deliberately pair media in line with the importance and priority of information: for example, send an email, then follow up with a text. This helps people to act on what is urgent and avoids long response times.

Of course, tech affects not just how we complete tasks but also how we connect, and this is a bigger challenge to overcome.

Leaders need to use digital tools to create relationships and connection, and to model engagement with others.

Use technology to connect people

Make sure you respond to people's contributions, ask follow-up questions, regularly schedule social interactions, pay attention to team dynamics and quickly surface the potential for discord. On page 75, I outlined the types of meetings that matter most, and these include personal check-ins and regular catchups that manage connection for both work and relationships.

An important leadership contribution is to make it easier for teams to connect across distance. Now more than ever, focus on connections that energise people.

Three key practices keep teams engaged:

1. **Structure in unstructured time** – so that there is spontaneous interaction. This could be a quick coffee, shared lunch break, happy hour or birthday celebration. Leaders need to initiate, turn up for and be part of these, encouraging informal, personal chat. Encourage team members to get together and check in with their peers and their own teams. Estimate how much time you spent doing this when you worked face-to-face, then replicate it.

2. **Emphasise individual differences** – ask everyone for their opinions and ensure equal turn taking. Avoid referring to people as members of subgroups; for example, 'what do the engineers think?', 'the team in Australia wants to…'. This can solidify the boundaries between different groups. Those boundaries already exist and can be harder to counteract remotely. Instead, focus on what unites people.

3. **Surface dissent** – it's even easier to avoid surfacing different perspectives, tensions and conflict when you work remotely. Instead, frame different perspectives and dissent as being positive to the work you do. Encourage 'devil's advocates' and take it in turn to play a devil's advocate role. Intentionally ask for divergent views and options. This normalises differences, frames them as helpful not harmful, and reduces conflict.

RESET YOUR WORK STRUCTURE

Doing what matters shouldn't be exhausting or boring: it should be inspiring and satisfying. Do a lovingly crafted job and collaborate meaningfully and productively with colleagues to achieve your most important work together.

To increase your flexAbility and help you love your work, create a structure that allows you to organise what to do, prioritise so that you do what's most important, and use digital tools to make it easier. To reset your work structure:

1. Craft your job; align it with your responsibilities, strengths, passions and motivations.

2. Ruthlessly assess your existing meetings, cut out the fat and set up a productive cadence of the meetings that matter most.

3. Prioritise your work using the Four Disciplines.

4. Choose the digital tools that make collaborative work easier and more engaging.

CHAPTER 5

DEEPEN YOUR FOCUS

'Disciplined attention is the currency of leadership.'
— Ronald Heifetz, Marty Linsky and Alexander Grashow[62]

Sofia was nearing her return-to-work date after major surgery, and was concerned about how she would respond to the level of demands she knew she'd face.

Like many leaders, Sofia had been caught in the trap of having her time consumed by 'shallow work'. The relentless schedule of meetings, interspersed by the constant pings of phone calls, texts and emails crowded out focus, concentration and work on the things that really mattered.

Her identity as a leader and a professional was intricately bound to her ability to work with complex concepts for which there were no easy answers. She was highly skilled at understanding and mediating between the competing positions of multiple powerful stakeholders. She was recognised for creating innovative solutions that had the support of those stakeholders and which gained accolades for herself and her organisation. Yet over time, she was aware she had less and less time to devote to these aspects of her work.

Sofia's return-to-work resolution was to make sure she prioritised her most important, and most fulfilling, work.

Even when we know what matters most to us, there may be many obstacles to getting it done. This chapter focuses on how to manage your attention so that you can routinely be as focused and productive as possible. For Sofia, having clarity of focus that served her purpose made it easier to realign her everyday routine so that it served rather than sabotaged her. She was able to increase how much time she spent doing deep, focused work.

Assess your focus

Start by assessing the quality of your focus:

1. How easily do you notice how you spend your time?

2. How well is your time aligned to your purpose and priorities?

3. How easily do you reorient your attention to focus on your priorities?

4. What are your best tactics for making sure you focus on what's most important to do?

5. What interferes most with being able to manage your attention and time as you would like to?

As attention is a critical currency for leadership, the first step is to ensure your attention is focused on what is most meaningful, rewarding and impactful. Easier said than done! Focus takes discipline and energy. However, it uses your energy in a positive way: if you manage your attention well, you can better moderate your mood and generate rather than sap your energy.

Most likely you can manage your attention when you have sufficient energy and feel a sense of agency. When your daily routine works well, it allows you to create a working rhythm which is energising, not depleting.

Figure 5 shows the accumulating power of managing your attention. Begin by intentionally stopping the automatic flow of thoughts and events and increase your awareness – what's called 'meta-attending'. Then you can unhook yourself from unhelpful thinking; psychological flexibility, discussed in Chapter 3, is the foundation for this. Once unhooked, you can connect to your purpose and realign. The fourth step is to prime yourself to switch to work that serves your purpose. Then, you can do focused work.

Figure 5: Five steps to deepen your focus

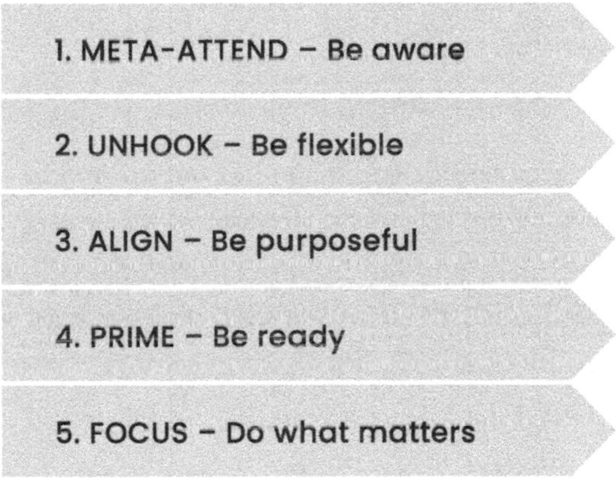

1. META-ATTEND – Be aware

2. UNHOOK – Be flexible

3. ALIGN – Be purposeful

4. PRIME – Be ready

5. FOCUS – Do what matters

In this chapter, we'll go through each of the five steps in detail. Once you're familiar with the steps, turn them into habits. There's enormous value in routine, and the more your routine is supported by habits that help you to do focused, quality work, the better. Chapter 6 will outline how to sync your focus practices into habits to make them routine.

1. Meta-attend: be aware

Back at work, Sofia assessed her attention and realised that she was getting too caught up in the flow of responding to expectations – both her own and others'. When she asked herself the assessment questions on page 86, she answered 'Somewhat' for her default self on the first three questions.

Careening from one online meeting to the next, as is so often the case, means good-quality thinking is put off. The expectation is that the thinking will happen later. However, what usually happens is:

a) the thinking does happen later, but it interferes with non-work life

b) the quality of the thinking is reduced because after a day full of meetings you're tired

c) it probably doesn't happen at all despite a) and b).

It wasn't that Sofia couldn't manage her attention and concentrate on good-quality thinking work. However, she wasn't pausing to make sure she spent enough time on it. In her willingness to do good work, she put herself in the cockpit of a fighter jet, when she needed to be in a 737. She needed to slow down and focus on the long haul.

There are five different forms of attention, according to Daniel Goleman and Richard Davidson:[63]

1. **selective attention** – being able to focus on one thing to the exclusion of others

2. **vigilance** – being able to maintain constant attention over time

3. **allocating attention** – being able to notice shifts in your attention

4. **goal focus or cognitive control** – being able to keep a specific task in focus, despite distractions

5. **meta-awareness** – being able to keep track of your awareness.

All these forms of awareness are important for doing focused work.

Meta-awareness is the most helpful form of attention, however, because it allows us to notice, monitor and refocus our attention.

Mindfulness, which I also mentioned in Chapter 3, is a foundation practice that will boost your ability to be aware of your attention and will support each of the five steps. This first step, 'Meta-attend', is to catch yourself in the act of not paying attention, of being on autopilot.

INSIGHT
Mindfulness increases focus and creates calm

Mindfulness involves training the mind to pay attention in a particular way. Psychologist and mindfulness expert Russ Harris defines it as 'paying attention with flexibility, openness, and curiosity.'[64]

There is a range of different mindfulness techniques, all of which are designed to increase three things:

1. paying attention to the present moment through the careful observation of perceptions, cognitions, emotions or sensations

2. the non-judgemental acceptance of all thoughts, feelings and experiences

3. managing the focus of your attention with ease and flexibility.

Mindfulness practices vary greatly in length and type: from brief one-minute activities (like the STOP exercise, overleaf), to spending 10 minutes being mindful of your breath, to 45-minute body scans.

The body scan is an exercise in which attention is directed sequentially to specific areas of the body; sensations in each area are carefully observed. In sitting exercises, participants are instructed to sit in a relaxed and wakeful posture with eyes closed and to direct attention to the sensations of breathing. You can also practice mindfulness during ordinary activities like walking, standing and eating.

When emotions, sensations or cognitions arise during a mindfulness practice, they are observed non-judgementally. When you notice that your mind has wandered into thoughts, memories or fantasies, briefly note the nature or content of them, if possible, and then return your attention to the present moment.

Even judgemental thoughts (for example, 'This is a foolish waste of time') should be observed non-judgementally. An important consequence is the realisation that most sensations, thoughts and emotions fluctuate – they come and go.

Focusing attention in this way is initially quite effortful. With practice, however, it becomes less so, until you achieve a form of 'effortless concentration'.

Mindfulness practices interrupt thinking and evaluation, and help us to let go of judgement.

A brief mindfulness practice, developed by Jon Kabat-Zinn and part of the Mindfulness-Based Stress Reduction approach, uses STOP as an acronym to take charge of your thinking. The word 'stop' is a great cue because its meaning is very clear. STOP is a cue to change your attention state. It gives you a moment to pause, and in that moment you can make different choices about how you proceed.

If you have trouble stopping and focusing your thinking, if time passes in a blur of activity and yet you haven't done the important things, try using the STOP acronym. Yes, it takes only one minute, and the payback for establishing this as a routine extends far beyond one minute!

How to STOP

1. Stop and interrupt your 'automatic pilot' by concentrating on the present moment.

2. Take a breath and bring your focus to the experience of the in-breath and the out-breath.

3. Open yourself to observation. Connect to the experience of this moment and inquire with a sense of curiosity:

   - What am I seeing?
   - What am I feeling?
   - What am I sensing?
   - What am I hearing?
   - What am I smelling?
   - What am I thinking?

4. Proceed to reconnect with your surroundings and with your activity in the moment.

Even short doses of mindfulness, like this one, improve attention. As mental training, mindfulness produces lasting changes in brain and cognitive function.

To turn mindfulness into a habit takes regular practice. You could set up calendar reminders several times a day so that you can practise STOP.

Another way to begin would be to practise STOP after each scheduled meeting in your day. Continue to schedule reminders and experiment with ways to practise STOP until it becomes ingrained.

2. Unhook: be flexible

Mindful thinking allows you to stay present in the moment with full awareness and openness. Once you've stopped your autopilot, you can open your thinking and give yourself the opportunity to rethink your choices.

Back in Chapter 3, Marlena found herself hooked. She was accepting all work requests to prove she was worthy of her job – she wasn't saying no because she believed doing so would give the impression that flexibility couldn't work. She needed to unhook from these thoughts, which were generating disappointment.

By taking time to identify their hooks and consider their impact, both Marlena and Sofia were able to:

1. question how workable the hooks were (Not very...)
2. become better at noticing when the hooks were affecting their choices
3. take alternative action and avoid their hooks in the future.

Clarifying and examining critical internal voices allows us to make choices about their value.

We all have critical inner voices. What matters most is their volume and how often they hook us and distract us from our goals. We can shift their influence over us, too. Using humour and reframing are two great tactics for minimising the inner critic, and are my personal favourites.

Using her psychological flexibility, open learning in particular, helped Sofia to unhook by discovering new tactics for managing her workload.

3. Align: be purposeful

Aligning is the third step in managing your attention focus. Chapter 2 has covered the important ground of why purpose matters so much to help us choose to be, and stay, flexAble.

Connect back to your purpose so that you can focus your attention where you need to.

4. Prime: be ready

Priming is a great tactic to help you make good choices about what you will do. Priming means to influence your own thinking in a particular way. You can create and rehearse cues that help you to focus your thoughts, feelings and actions. These simple cues then act as primes, so that when you go into a situation or conversation you are more likely to say and do what you intend to. Repeat your values and your purpose until you're able to produce them 'on demand' to make them easier to access. Sofia used a sticky note, 'FOCUS', on her computer as her cue.

When well-primed, you are more likely to do your focused work.

5. Focus: do what matters

Sofia and her team were tasked with important knowledge work. They needed to produce innovative yet practical recommendations about future scenarios that would engage a diverse range of stake-holders. And they needed a routine that supported the creation of that kind of work. Despite this being their priority, the biggest challenge Sofia experienced was having adequate time to do it.

This kind of work is what author and computer science Professor Cal Newport calls 'deep work'. Newport's definition of deep work is 'Professional activities performed in a state of distraction-free concentration that push your cognitive capabilities to the limit. These efforts create new value, improve your skill, and are hard to replicate'.[65]

One of the biggest challenges to focusing on meaningful, 'deep' work is that we simply have less willpower than we think we do.

Newport suggests that rather than relying on willpower, you should set yourself up for deep work. It's helpful to have a 'philosophy' for your deep work that fits into your specific circumstances, to increase your success. Possible philosophies include:

- **being monastic** – cutting yourself off from the world as much as possible

- **using bimodal scheduling** – clearly dividing your time between concentrated periods of deep work, ranging from a full day to weeks or months, and engaging in 'shallow work' as normal at other times

- **having a rhythm** – doing an amount of deep work each day, scheduled in your diary and with a consistent starting time

- **being journalistic** – fitting deep work in whenever your schedule allows.

While the monastic approach is the philosophy that yields the biggest benefits, it is by far the hardest to organise and the least realistic for most people. Increased working from home provides – at least in theory – a greater opportunity to experiment with the remaining three philosophies.

Those with family responsibilities, with children who are being schooled or cared for at home, or whose home working spaces are shared, may find any of these philosophies difficult to do. Aiming for a bimodal schedule – for example, going into the office to do concentrated work in a quiet space – could be the more workable approach.

Sofia opted for a combination of bimodal and rhythmic scheduling. She set aside Fridays for dedicated deep work and advised her teams that she was not contactable then unless there was an emergency. As her teams' work generally didn't require a crisis response, this was feasible for her.

She also set aside time for deep work in her schedule between 10.30 a.m. and 12.30 p.m. on Mondays, Tuesdays and Thursdays.

At the beginning of each week, she reviewed her work program, leadership obligations and general commitments. Occasionally she needed to adjust her deep-work time to better suit work expectations.

Along with setting time aside when she was unavailable to others, Sofia also set up clear times when she welcomed team-member contact. Her daily routine began with a quick check-in with her team leaders so that they had access to her and they could jointly consider priorities and issues. She finished her day with a quick ring-around to her team leaders to acknowledge their work and stay in touch with how they were feeling.

The journalistic philosophy – fitting in deep work whenever you can – is the most difficult to follow. However, it's still worth trying if your schedule is demanding and you are unable to tightly manage it – say, for example, you have children and only ad hoc or intermittent childcare. Being clear about what work you need to complete in a deep way and priming for it will help you to use the moments opportunistically.

To support deep work, it helps to have a location for it. It might not be realistic for you, but keeping the same place for your deep work is helpful. It might be your office or a corner of your dining room – putting up a do-not-disturb sign might be the indicator to both you and others that you are in deep-work mode.

Using a specific timeframe is also best, as Sofia did with her two-hourly slots.

Deep work doesn't include checking email or social media, so turn off your notifications, close web browsers and avoid manual checking. Consider disconnecting from the internet if temptation is too strong.

The Pomodoro technique is a great option to help you be productive during the time you set aside. It's simple: once you've decided on your task, set a timer for 25 minutes and work in as focused a way as possible for those 25 minutes. Take a five-minute break, then set the timer again. After four 25-minute sessions, take a longer break. You can find out more at en.wikipedia.org/wiki/Pomodoro_Technique.

Also consider using a particular metric to support your deep work, such as the number of words per half-hour or pages produced per session.

A final tip is to think about your rituals for starting and finishing deep work – such as getting a cup of coffee, using a particular notebook dedicated to deep work or having your workspace arranged in a particular 'deep work' mode.

Structuring your work like this gives it weight and meaning, and you increase the importance of it. This helps to stop procrastination and to motivate you.

Focus your collaboration

So far in this chapter I've been discussing individual deep work, but collaborative deep work may also be part of your role. If this is the case, use the steps in this chapter as a guide to identify how to work side by side with others to generate more valuable outputs.

One of the concerns people raise about remote work is that the opportunity for 'random creativity' is lost. The belief that watercooler conversations lead to some of the best decisions and insights remains prevalent. This was the view back in 2013 when

Yahoo banned working from home: being in the office was considered essential for spontaneous collaboration and innovation.

Ethan S. Bernstein says that not only is there no evidence to support this view, one of the major innovations designed to increase collaboration – the open-plan office – in fact decreases collaboration. Despite being closer together, people in open-space offices actually have fewer face-to-face interactions.[66] Too much collaboration causes resistance; the more we try to make people work together, the less they do. What's more, the research shows that their decisions get worse.

What Bernstein's research shows is that there needs to be a particular rhythm to collaborative work.[67]

Solving problems collaboratively requires two different sets of activities: gathering information and deciding.

Information-gathering benefits from high levels of connectivity to work out who's doing what; it needs good coordination to ensure that a wide range of information is covered and to avoid duplication of effort.

Deciding needs imagination, and that is undermined by too much connectedness. When everyone is deciding together, too often consensus is prioritised over a quality decision, and the loudest voices prevail. When people work together intermittently rather than constantly, they have more opportunity to process information for themselves, and to learn and experiment. Then, when they get together, they have a range of different views that they can work on. Collaborative intelligence is more likely.

RESET YOUR FOCUS

The practices outlined in this chapter help you to plan and review your work, and to improve your focus. Focus on the work that matters most to you and create a system which makes best use of your time and your mental energy. You may not do deep work each day, but if it is scheduled, you stand a better chance of doing it.

Save your brainpower for where it really counts, where it would have most value and where you would feel most satisfaction – make it a priority to do the deep work you need to do.

Use the five-step reset process described in this chapter to create clearer focus, increase your concentration and do the work that matters most. To recap:

1. Stop default thinking. Meta-attend.

2. Get off the hook, let go of unhelpful thoughts and feelings and consider new possibilities.

3. Align with purpose. Remind yourself of what is most important to you.

4. Prime yourself. Don't stay in the slipstream of distractions or automatic thoughts. Be deliberate and ready to turn your intentions into action.

5. Focus on what matters most. Embed deep-work practices to do your best work.

CHAPTER 6

MAKE IT STICK

'[L]ife meaning is a lofty notion tied to spirituality, love, and great accomplishment. But habits provide a quieter bedrock of such meaning.' – Wendy Wood[68]

At the start of Chapter 5, Sofia was about to return to work after extended leave. She reflected that before her surgery, she'd been feeling stressed. So, before heading back into the fray, she wanted to find ways to keep her sense of purpose and avoid slipping back into the same old unhelpful habits. She wanted to be better at managing her stress and anxiety levels, to avoid any deterioration in her wellbeing.

With her wellbeing an even more important priority than it had been pre-surgery, she was more motivated to develop a better routine. She needed to be focused to meet the demands of her work but also to stay well.

Sofia reviewed the way she managed her focus and increased her mindfulness practices. She was clearer about both her purpose and priorities and knew how to get more high-quality knowledge work done. Now, somehow, she needed to make these new practices stick.

Having clarity of focus helped Sofia to know how to increase the amount and quality of important, versus urgent, work. The next step was to turn her new work intentions into habits. The habits would, in turn, create a routine that would serve her purpose and ease the flow of her working days.

Like most people, Sofia thought that prioritising her work and then executing as planned was a matter of willpower. She wished she had a bit more willpower and could rely on it a bit more often! It was a relief to learn that it's not a lack of willpower that keeps people locked into unhelpful behaviour but a lack of habits aligned with priorities.

Appreciating that meant that she could stop beating herself up for not having enough willpower – she had ample! Once her renewed practices were habits, they would become automatic and she could devote more time to the work that mattered.

This chapter will help you create a routine of the right habits.

Assess your work habits

Start with an assessment of how well you believe you're managing your work habits right now:

1. How in control do you feel of your daily schedule and working pattern?
2. How aware are you of the habits that currently get you through your day?
3. How well does your routine work for you: does it give you the level of flexAbility you seek?
4. What gets in the way of achieving a good working day?

5. What interferes most with being able to manage your time as you would like to?

Habits reduce the number of decisions you need to make throughout your day. They help reduce variance and distraction, and stop you from wasting energy making minor, unimportant decisions. Having a routine for your work means you make it easy to be as productive as possible, as often as possible. That reduces the friction you feel in your day and, importantly, reduces cognitive load.

Establishing a routine helps to align your best intentions with what you do. The more your day is powered by habits that align with your purpose and values, the more energy you will feel, the more congruence you will achieve and the easier your work will flow.

It might seem counter-intuitive that habits and routine help you to lead flexAbly. Not so! You increase flexAbility by locking the right practices into your routine.

INSIGHT

Habits, not willpower, embed new routines

Getting the right practices to stick is not about exerting willpower or being a 'good' person. It's about identifying the behaviours you want to do routinely, then turning them into habits.

According to Wendy Wood,[69] we harbour the mistaken belief that it is our willpower that is responsible for what we do. We think that if we can properly harness that, then we'll do the right thing. Exerting willpower, however, is extremely draining. If we rely on it to help us to do what's right, we will almost certainly fail. Those people who live their lives consistently with their purpose are not better at exerting their willpower: they are better at establishing good habits.

If you rely on your willpower to get your exercise done, for example – say, each morning you struggle with yourself to get out of bed and do 30 minutes of exercise – you have expended a great deal of mental energy even before you've started the exercise. Debating with yourself or cajoling yourself to get up *now* takes energy. Even when you are committed to it.

As Wendy Wood says, successful change is not marked by personal fortitude or determination. Being clear about your goals, taking simple steps, organising the context around you and encouraging enjoyable actions is what successful people do.

She says that 'Until we have laid down a habit in neural networks and memory systems, we must wilfully decide to repeat a new action again and again, even when it's a struggle. At some point, it becomes second nature, and we can sit back and let autopilot drive'.[70]

Disrupt unhelpful habits and routines

You need to adjust your everyday routine to make sure what you do is in service to your purpose.

Embedding what matters most in habits makes it so much easier to do. It frees up conscious resources to make bigger decisions, to do deep work and to lead well.

Habits are neither good nor bad: the question is how well they serve you. Do they allow you to do what matters? Or do your habits sabotage your purpose and goals, having you routinely doing things you know don't matter much or wasting time on things that you don't even want to do (hint – social media)?

When we are most stressed, it is our habits, good or bad, that get us through. When we experience a threat, our rational, conscious decision-making processes tend to shut down. In other words, when we most need our full brainpower, it's less available.

Because we have less brainpower available, what come to the fore are habits – the behaviour that requires the least effort.

If our habits are in line with our purpose and goals, then even under pressure they help us to respond at our best. They buoy us up, rather than weighing us down. They help us to feel familiarity, predictability, safety and fluency. We haven't avoided threat and stress, but we have accessed our better selves.

The automaticity of habits is both an upside and a downside. It's great when a habit is positive, but less helpful when a habit we are no longer aware of is getting in our way. Given that something like 43 per cent of our behaviour is habitual, there is plenty of scope for examination.[71]

Start by reviewing what your habits are now. You need a way to expose habits, consider their value, identify unhelpful habits and stop or replace them. Sofia's break from her work provided a discontinuity that helped her do that. At first it led to her feeling confused, but it also highlighted what she was taking for granted.

If you don't have an existing review practice, take yourself to a new place or connect with a peer, coach or mentor to help yourself notice what you are doing. New contexts and new relationships invariably provoke new perspectives – the disruption of moving house or office is a good example. A disruption is anything that makes it harder to repeat what you are doing, and this is positive when you are seeking to make a change (but less so when you want to maintain habits). Feeling a sense of dissatisfaction with your routine, or feeling that you can't seem to get enough done, are good cues that you need to disrupt your existing habits.

Reviewing the 43 per cent of our behaviours governed by habit allows us to make choices to bring them into line with our purpose and goals.

Having reviewed your habits, now set goals to help you make your desired change. Goals are the conscious effort needed to help you build a desirable habit. You need to create the goal, manage your context, get a procedure in place, then practise it for two to three months until it becomes automatic. The more complex the behaviour you want to change, the longer it will take to become habitual.

The more friction there is between you and your goal, the more work you will need to do to establish your habit; reduce the friction, as you can, to make it easier. The biggest source of friction is your context. Your context creates cues for your behaviour – and cues are easier to notice than the habit, so they become good triggers.

The louder the behavioural cues, the more your context is aligned with your new goal, and the quicker it will embed as habit. For example, if your alarm is your cue to get up and exercise, that's nice and clear.

In families, it might not be so easy to change your context and you might not have such a degree of control over the cues around you. When many people are involved in a decision, it's harder. So, set up shared cues where you can do activities with others in your family, and create virtuous habits together.

Using habit sequences or stacks – chunking a series of habits to be done together – is a great tactic. When you repeat an activity with several components and continue to do them in the same way each time, your brain treats the sequence as one activity. That reduces cognitive load.

Variety, on the other hand, weakens habit. If you can reduce variety (for example, by doing the same thing each day), it will be easier to create your habit. If it's too boring, though, it might not hold your attention, so balance routine repetitiveness with creative, stimulating activities. For example, you may want to exercise more, and you know that going for a 20-minute run will give you the best benefit. But you find running boring. Create your goal for the number of days or amount of time you exercise, but vary the activity; for example, alternate running and power-walking, or vary your route to increase interest.

To help build a habit, you need a reward – a dopamine hit – to immediately follow your desired activity. Rewards include congratulating yourself when you complete your exercise, treating yourself to your favourite coffee or simply feeling invigorated – even virtuous – when you finish. The greater the time lag between the activity and the reward, the less likely it is that a link will be created between them. Repeating the behaviour and experiencing the reward is an investment in embedding the behaviour and locking in a habit. When the reward no longer matters to you, the habit has been formed.

Build the habits for a good daily routine

My habit framework in Figure 6 overleaf provides a structure to review your existing work habits and identify opportunities to improve your daily routine. The framework creates a focus on three times when habits generally make the biggest difference to your day – the start, middle and end. This is represented on the vertical dimension of the framework.

The horizontal dimension comprises three major perspectives leaders need to manage throughout their day. We tend to think about what we do from the perspective of 1) our self and what's important to us, 2) our role as leaders and 3) the work that needs to be done.

Together, the two dimensions create a 3 × 3 matrix, giving you nine areas to consider. Identify where you have a crunch or a gap in your existing habits and prioritise those areas for focus. If you'd like to work through all nine areas, start with the top left square, 'Prime', and get that sorted, then move on to 'Pause' and 'Close'. Once you have the 'Self' column covered, move to 'Lead'.

Figure 6: Habits for a good daily routine

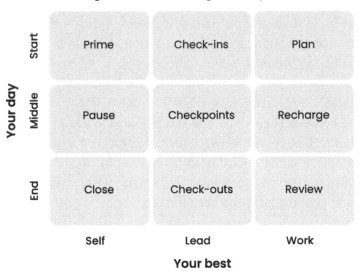

Let's look at the nine areas in detail, now.

Prime

Research by Jinshil Hyun and colleagues confirms what we know intuitively: waking up on the wrong side of the bed is a guarantee for a bad day![72] Their research concluded that if you start your day thinking about how stressful it will be, your working memory, which helps you to learn and retain information, is lowered during the day. Performance decreases. If you start your day by thinking it will be stressful, you will feel a stress effect even if nothing stressful ends up happening.

Anticipating stressful events has the same effect on working memory as experiencing the events. More than that, reduced working memory increases the chances of making mistakes and decreases your focus.

Interestingly, stress anticipation from the previous evening doesn't affect working memory in the same way: it's your morning mindset that matters the most.

So, make sure you get a good start to your day; it pays off. Priming your morning mindset sets you up to have a good day.

A positive morning mindset is a strong foundation to help you work at your peak during the day.

Begin your day by using positive priming. What are your current habits for starting your day? Check to make sure your habits set up your morning mindset positively. Establish a routine of habits that help you to start the day with positive thoughts about the day, and clear intentions about what you will achieve.

Doing mindfulness or relaxation practices and exercise can help you to feel positive and reduce the distraction of negative thoughts. If negative thoughts arise about your day – for example, you have a meeting scheduled that you have been dreading – mindfully let those feelings go, distract yourself from them through activity and keep moving through your routine.

The idea of positively 'reattaching' to work, proposed by Sabine Sonnentag, is another practice to consider for getting the day off to a good start.[73] Rather than drifting or catapulting into your work, actively reattach to it. This is particularly important if/when you work from home, as the transition from non-work to work may be less tangible.

Try these three ways to 'reattach' to your work each morning. Remind yourself of:

1. **why the work you do matters to you** – how does your work impact the lives of others? What's your sense of purpose? What are your goals?

2. **your supporters** – who are the people, both at work and outside, who care about your professional success?

3. **your focus for the day** – what is a specific goal or task that you would like to complete? Visualise yourself doing it in a calm and focused way.

How do you tune in and mentally prepare yourself for a good day at work?

Create a 'best you' morning habit stack. Remember that a habit stack is a combined sequence of habits that makes it easier to do them. Ideally, work your way back from your work starting time to your waking time and put together the habits that will help you to get set up for your best day experience. Schedule waking up at a regular time, exercise, mindfulness and reattachment practices.

One of the biggest challenges to having your own good habits, of course, is other people and their habits! Helping others in your household to establish good morning habits will be a bonus for them as well as you. It might not be easy, and it might be that you can't run your morning in your ideal way, but do what you can to make it easier for yourself to commit to your own priority habits.

Pause

The practice of taking a lunch break, or even of allowing breaks between meetings, has decreased dramatically. Yet taking breaks during your day helps you to maintain your energy, stay focused and perform better. You need to pause during the day to give your brain and body the opportunity to recharge – I've discussed this in some detail in Chapter 1.

Positive psychologists Shawn Achor and Michelle Gielan suggest we need to think differently about how resilience works.[74] Resilience isn't about enduring more but about how you recharge – and the key to resilience is being able to recharge more. Rather than trying to keep pushing through your day and then using your leisure time to recover, recharge through the day. Paradoxically, trying hard to overcome low energy exacerbates exhaustion.

Recharge, even if you don't think you need it. That way you will feel less depleted and finish your workday feeling refreshed.

The harder you work, the more recovery you need to stay resilient. To make sure you recharge during your day, focus on short five- to ten-minute periods of relaxation during the day that give you a cognitive break. Remember from Chapter 1, you create cognitive breaks when you shift your attention, change work tasks, step away from work when your energy drops, go for a short walk or have a warm conversation.

As we saw in Chapter 4, a rhythm of continuous meetings without breaks has become an unfortunate habit for many. You could try to reduce your meeting times, and use the time in between meetings for brief cognitive breaks. Try a short mindfulness practice between the end of one meeting and the start of the next, as suggested in Chapter 5, page 89. If the meetings are via remote means, stand up and stretch for a couple of minutes between them.

Plan regular breaks in your day, make them habitual and use them to build your resilience.

Close

The 'Close' area of the habit framework refers to explicitly ending your working day. Psychological detachment – a full switching off from work – is necessary for recovering from work.[75] I discussed this briefly in Chapter 1. The more intense your cognitive activity, the greater the mental fatigue. Working long hours comes with serious penalties: it doesn't only erode productivity, it also robs you of recovery and leisure time.

How do you usually end your working day? How well does it help your psychological detachment? Is there room for improvement?

One of the challenges some people find with remote work from home is managing the boundaries between work and non-work. Having a ritual for closing out your workday, comprising small habits, can be effective: designate a particular time to finish the day, and schedule a calendar reminder.

Some people find real benefit in travelling from their workplace to home. If you commute, use the time to decompress, listen to music or observe what's going on in the world around you. When working from home, create a substitution for a 'commute' ritual, such as going for a walk. Shut down your computer to end the day and to make restarting later in the evening more difficult. Change from work wear to casual wear, start to prepare the evening meal, spend time with family or do some exercise.

Another ritual for closing out the day is to use a 'daily diary' system. Ask yourself three questions about a current goal, and write the answers in a diary or notebook. This is a mini-reflection and helps to boost your motivation, too! The questions are:

1. What did I do today to progress my goal? (e.g. type of work, focus, recharging)
2. What got in the way of making progress on my goal?

3. What do I need to do tomorrow to make progress on my goal?

The intention is to notice progress, even very small amounts of it. Be positive and focus on what you have done; don't be critical or concerned with what you haven't done.

Check-ins, checkpoints and check-outs

The habits that help you to be at your best underpin the work you do as leader. Review how you check in with your team at key points during the day; it helps to have a structure and cadence to it, and Chapter 4 provides some suggestions. One thing people really need from their leaders, especially when things are complex and dynamic, is consistency. Establish patterns of engagement with your team to help them get off to a good start and stay focused and motivated. Help them to detach from work at the end of the day, as well.

Consistent team habits help everyone to do the right thing, and they help to manage motivation and emotional connection. Again, there are other suggestions on what to do in Chapter 4. Choose what is going to have most value for your team, and then lock it into the routine. Check-ins, checkpoints and check-outs serve to focus both work effort and emotional engagement, so create your routine to encompass this broad range of practices. Identify what sorts of checks need to be done daily, weekly and monthly, and what their focus will be.

Spending regular time with your people helps you to be aware if they are struggling: you can monitor their wellbeing, help them balance work and life demands and provide coaching and support. Doing this frequently in shorter bursts is better than less often in longer bursts. It also gives you the opportunity to provide regular recognition and acknowledge achievements.

Finally, make sure that some of the checks are focused on increasing the social life and engagement of the team.

Plan, recharge, review

The final column of the habits framework is 'Work', comprising 'Plan', 'Recharge' and 'Review'. You can use a system like this to help you focus on your new habits, as well as to focus on helping the team do the work they need to do.

How you designate the 'start' and 'close' of the day might vary according to people's working arrangements and locations – use the terms as metaphors rather than prescriptions.

Help people set up for productive working days by making it easy for them to know what work they need to do and how to achieve the right work standards.

Alongside that, make sure there are plenty of touchpoints to keep you connected, give people human access to you and ensure they aren't overloaded.

Embed deep-work habits

Embed your deep-work approach from Chapter 5 to plan, recharge and review your productivity during the day. To make high-quality, productive work easier and more satisfying, identify when and how in your day you do your best deep work. As we discussed in Chapter 5, focus on the work that matters most to you and create a system to make best use of your mental energy.

You may not do it every day, but if time for deep work is scheduled, you stand a better chance of producing it. Scheduling helps you create the right habits, and habits create a sense of comfort and 'fit'. This doesn't mean, however, that you need to schedule every moment of your life, nor should you be too concerned if occasionally the routine doesn't work or isn't helpful. Is it time for a tweak? Tweak away. Slipped up today? No problem, get back into it tomorrow.

Your habits help you to establish your routine. The repetition of habitual practices is hugely rewarding.

Use rituals to embed routines

As you develop a routine that works for you, add one further element: rituals. Rituals are regular acts that capture spiritual meaning which gives them greater power. Rituals are a universal human impulse; they calm fear and anxiety and convey comfort. A series of habits can become a ritual through repetition, and by giving them special meaning.

Priming your day and closing out your day may become important rituals. As a part of priming your day, you could use an initiating ritual – for example, using a certain notebook, setting up a timer or opening a particular tab in your browser. Performing the ritual stops distraction and has a symbolic association with getting started.

Rituals are especially important when we face loss, are undergoing difficulties or have something particularly challenging, like deep work, to do. They are soothing and create a sense of control.

What seems to be most important is labelling what you do a 'ritual'. Tell yourself, 'This is my ritual for getting started each day', 'This is our ritual for how we conduct our meetings', 'This is our ritual for closing the day'. Use the word to get the benefit.

With increased working from home, rituals that help mark a change from work to non-work are especially important.

RESET YOUR HABITS

With clarity of focus and effort, you can create great habits and routines that help you to feel fulfilled and satisfied. And with the right habits locked in, you can achieve the flexAbility you seek.

Review your existing habits, put together a routine of new and improved habits, name your rituals and get yourself on track to produce your best work, flexAbly.

1. Review your habits. Identify those that help and those that hold you back.

2. Make your day work better for you by fine-tuning your morning mindset, recharging through the day and explicitly closing out of work mode.

3. Structure check-ins, checkpoints and check-outs to help your team get off to a good start, stay focused and then detach at the end of the day.

4. Establish deep-work habits to make high-quality, productive work easier and more satisfying.

5. Use a daily diary to review your progress, identify what gets in your way and adjust as needed.

6. Lock your routine in by embedding rituals that create a sense of control and comfort.

PART III

Influence what matters

*'Great leaders are awake, aware, and attuned
to themselves, to others, and to the world around them.
They commit to their beliefs, stand strong in their
values, and live full, passionate lives.'*
They are mindful, hopeful and compassionate.

RICHARD BOYATZIS AND ANNIE MCKEE[76]

YOU CAN increase your flexAbility by getting more work done through others. It's not about shifting the burden but about lightening the load – for everyone. It's about reducing resistance, getting buy-in and increasing your influence. Influencing to increase your impact is the focus for Part III.

Chapter 7 focuses on how to increase the variety of the leadership influencing styles you use to achieve outcomes. Influence is not about having a single, go-to style: it's about being able to choose from a range of styles and adapt your approach to different situations. The more styles you can use, the more flexAbly, the less friction there is and the quicker the result.

Getting more done, but doing less of it yourself, is the sweet spot for influencing. More delegation is what it takes. Chapter 8 presents a framework for increasing your delegation, making it simpler and easier for you to delegate. The more you can delegate, the fewer hours you need to work. Delegation isn't about slacking off, though, and it isn't about exploiting others either. It requires a tight regime of good leading – safety, trust, recognition and feedback. When your team is filled with highly capable, autonomous workers, you win and they win.

Finally, we bring it all together in Chapter 9, in which you'll learn how to strengthen your impact on others using your story. When you believe in yourself and convey your story with presence, you create a resonance between yourself and others. You increase your leadership impact, making it easier to mobilise others around you and inspire them. Using your story, you can gain advocates who will help you prevent overwork, beat burnout and enjoy more freedom at work.

CHAPTER 7

FLEX YOUR STYLE

'Before people decide what they think of your message,
they decide what they think of you.'
— Amy Cuddy, Matthew Kohut and John Neffinger[77]

The end of his first 90 days in his new leadership role was approaching and Rafiq wasn't where he had planned to be. His progress with two of his teams was as expected, but his third team was proving to be hard work.

Rafiq had expected this team to be more challenging, because it hadn't been performing as expected previously. To get on top of the issues as quickly as possible, Rafiq had thought through the approach he wanted to take. He'd met with the team leader and held a couple of team meetings to introduce himself and get to know them, then focused in on what was going wrong. He'd made it clear to the team leader that the performance issues that were holding the team back needed to be resolved.

Rafiq found himself working longer and harder, yet the problem wasn't improving. He was frustrated. Enjoyment in his work was diminishing, his pride in his promotion was waning and he was feeling a bit awkward about what he would say in his next one-to-one with his CEO. He wasn't having the influence he needed to have – and his reputation was on the line.

When the going gets tough, we often default to getting tougher too. Rafiq had fallen into a classic leadership trap: focusing on the work that had to be done, rather than on the people who needed to do the work. He emphasised competence rather than warmth, relying on a persuasive leadership style with the team. He had translated his CEO's message into needing to exert control to resolve 'the problem', and this approach was backfiring.

A key challenge for leaders is how to exert personal authority to have the greatest influence. The usual mistake is to treat influence as a matter of quantity, when it's a matter of style. The best way to exercise authority is to flexibly adapt your style to the circumstances – and warm styles of engagement are much more important than we realise. To get his work and life back on track, Rafiq needed to do some flexAble thinking about what it meant to be a good leader, and to reset how he engaged with the team.

This chapter introduces you to a different way of thinking about influence. Influencing is, of course, critical for flexAble leaders; to prevent overwork and rework, you want to get the most done with the least effort. The easier it is to get others to do the work that needs doing, the better. The chapter outlines how you can achieve this by increasing the flexAbility of your influencing style.

Assess your influencing style

Take some time now to review your influencing style/s and your flexAbility:

1. How intentional are your tactics and style when you attempt to influence others?

2. How much do you rely on warmth when you influence others?

3. How readily do you adapt your influencing style to the situation and your relationships with the people you are influencing?

4. How satisfied are you with your influencing?

5. What's the most important thing that you need to focus on to improve your influence?

For a more comprehensive assessment, you can take my 'Influencing Style' quiz, which you'll find on my FlexAbility Resources webpage (www.karenmorley.com.au/flexability-resources).

To influence, show you care

What did you learn from your assessment of your influencing styles? If you believe that you would benefit from improving your influencing, or would like to increase the flexibility of your style, read on to find out how you can take your influence to the next level.

Interpersonal influence is the conscious manoeuvring of your behaviour to get the response you want from others. It doesn't get more important than this for leaders!

> **The more you show people you care,**
> **the easier it is to be an influential leader.**
> **That means you do less overwork.**

Empathy is fundamental to connecting and relationship-building. Despite rhetoric that emphasises taking charge and competitiveness, what we know about leadership influence is that you need to start with warmth.

Warmth and competence are the two key criteria by which we judge others. Research over decades by social psychologists Amy Cuddy, Susan Fiske and Peter Glick shows that these two attributes matter the most.[78] They're core to human interactions and fundamental to leading. They underpin effective influencing.

Professors Andrea Abele and Bogdan Wojciszke found that when we judge ourselves, we emphasise competence, yet when we judge others, we put warmth first.[79] We can use this awareness to influence more effectively: if you want to influence the people around you, you need to understand what motivates them, rather than what motivates you.

How warmth and competence go together matters for influencing. Putting competence first undermines trust, increases competitiveness and creates envy. Too much warmth without competence leads to pity; and when there's neither competence nor trust, contempt is the result. We most admire those leaders who start with warmth and then prove their competence. Their combination of warm confidence and calmness best projects a sense of trustworthy authority.

INSIGHT
Warmth and inspiration increase your influence

Most definitions of leadership have influencing at their core. Yet surprisingly little attention is paid to what influence is and what makes it effective for leaders.

There's a common misconception that influence is power, persuasion or manipulation. In reality, research by Chloe Bilton and Aaron Pincus[80] has shown that warm behaviours are much more influential.

They argue that we need to improve our understanding of what influence is and how it works.

Did you know the style of influence leaders use is a critical factor in whether people quit their jobs? A large-scale survey of 10,000 people found that 42 per cent had left their job because of dissatisfaction with their boss. In another, one-third of senior executives indicated that unhappiness with management was the main cause of top performer turnover. A Gallup meta-analysis of exit interview data showed that poor management features in 75 per cent of the reasons why people quit their jobs.[81]

Further, Christopher Reina and his colleagues found that specific influencing behaviours impact people's choice to stay or go. When leaders use tactics designed to inspire, it decreases people's intentions to leave. Pressure tactics, including disrespectful and abusive behaviour, dramatically increase people's intention to leave the organisation. In their research, a one-unit increase in pressure tactics was associated with a 91 per cent increase in intention to go, while a one-unit increase in inspiration led to a 68 per cent decrease in intention to go.

Leaders' actions shape how employees experience their workplace. They affect their level of engagement, and this plays a major role in how emotionally invested people are in their work. How leaders choose to influence has a significant impact on whether and how people participate. Leaders and organisations tend to be heavy-handed when it comes to influence, and so they are losing talent. This is not just costly, it's unnecessary.

Rafiq had emphasised his status without having much in the way of relationship capital. He was leading with competence – instead of first creating connections with others by showing he cared about their needs and interests. He needed to be able to create and maintain warm connections with them despite his new status.

This is a common mistake: leaders typically emphasise their competence or expertise with others. It makes sense: that's why you've been promoted, after all! However, you need to achieve the right blend of warmth with competence, relationship with task, so that people will follow your lead. Warmth comes first, because people:

- prefer to feel pleasure than pain or threat when they interact. When we are warm towards others, we are more pleasant to be with.

- like to feel a sense of hope rather than dread when they anticipate the future. When we offer hope to others, it gives them a sense of agency that makes putting in effort seem worthwhile.

- need to feel a sense of belonging – until we have that, we don't connect. Feeling accepted creates belonging, which is fundamental to our social survival and psychological wellbeing.

Pleasure, hope and acceptance are the motivations at the heart of influence. What Rafiq had not realised was that he was evoking dread about the future in his team ('Will I still have a job?') and a sense of rejection ('Do I really matter here?'). He needed to set aside his own agenda and sense of urgency to hook into the motivational states he wanted to evoke in others.

Five tactics guaranteed to boost your influence

The three motivations – pleasure, hope and acceptance – sit at the heart of five tactics that Tali Sharot explores in her book *The Influential Mind: What the brain reveals about our power to change others*.[82] Here are the five tactics:

1. Start with warmth, not facts.

2. Connect with others.

3. Avoid fear: it freezes.

4. Increase agency.

5. Now share facts.

1. Start with warmth, not facts

The most common mistake we make when we try to influence others is to wield facts. The challenge is that sharing your facts with others who have different views won't motivate the action you seek.

If we believe something, we find it hard to comprehend that others don't also believe it. We find our own knowledge and beliefs appealing and expect that others will too – and we get a burst of pleasure when we tell others our opinion or provide them with information. But that's not how it works for them. Starting with facts ('what I know', 'what you should believe', 'what I want you to do') tends to entrench people's existing beliefs. If they have no emotional investment in you or your logic, they may rationalise your position away.

Worse, when presented with facts counter to those they believe in, people are motivated to seek out confirmation of what they already know. They create counterarguments, causing a boomerang effect. They find new facts to invalidate or counteract yours to confirm their own.

> **The currency our brains use to assess new data and make decisions – emotion – is very different from the currency we believe our brains should use – logic.**

The use of logic ignores motives, fears, hopes and desires. This is why people's established beliefs and practices are very resistant to change despite the logic of new information. So, what we need to do to influence others is to create an emotional reaction.

2. Connect with others

Use warmth to create a personal connection, show you care and spend time understanding the other person at a human level. Then you can understand and address their needs and motivations.

Start by managing your own emotions. Focus on creating a positive connection: be optimistic, calm, and share a joke if that's appropriate. Manage any feelings of impatience.

Emotion is contagious: it transfers between us. When we show warmth and empathy to others, we create a reciprocal response, as we unconsciously mimic the emotions of others. Strong appeals to emotions and powerful speeches can cause our brains to 'click together'. In other words, people feel the same response no matter their personality or experiences: they feel like they 'click'. When they click, people process information in the same way and are more likely to agree.

It's important at this stage to put aside areas of disagreement, of which there may be many, to focus on areas of agreement. Finding common motivations, what unites us, is important to do first.

People approach what's pleasurable, and they will stay with something if it stays pleasurable. If it feels rewarding to be involved, they will be.

3. Avoid fear: it freezes

If our attempts to influence others evoke a fear response, then people freeze. Rafiq, for example, started with facts and logic without a pre-existing warm relationship with his team, and that meant that he created a fear response. The team leader told Rafiq that the team felt he misunderstood them and would restructure them. They dreaded this and so froze, avoided conversations with him and didn't share information.

The prospect of an uncertain future can cause avoidance. The more uncertain the future, the more we tend to avoid it and focus on what is rewarding for us right now. Warnings and threats also limit people's sense of control and take away their sense of agency. That works if what you want is inaction, but not if you want people to do something, or to change.

4. Increase agency

If you want people to be influenced by you, make it rewarding for them. Expect a better future and emphasise what needs to be done to achieve it. Give them a sense of agency and control.

Rafiq thought that leadership was all about exercising his authority – and yes, he did have authority and status. What was important, though, was how he wielded it. To be most effective and to achieve the outcomes he sought, he needed to give up his sense of 'being in control'. Many leaders feel this need to exert control; unfortunately, it's often experienced by others as micromanagement.

You can overcome the instinct to control and increase the control that others feel by giving them choice. Being able to choose is enjoyable: we love having choices.

Having a choice, even if it's small, gives people a sense of control, which is motivating. Giving people responsibility and reminding them that they have a choice increases their wellbeing.

However, too much choice can be overwhelming, so offer two or three options. Tali Sharot provides the example of the choices you might give to a kid who is a picky eater.[83] Offering them a choice of which green vegetable to eat – broccoli, beans or cabbage, for example – gives them ownership of the decision.

Rafiq thought about what choices he could offer. To restart his approach with the team, he asked them to choose when and where they met, and which coffee shop they would take their break in. This shifted the emotional dynamic: they laughed and joked with each other about the best time of day and who preferred which kind of coffee. It relieved some tension and started their meeting with a lighter touch.

Next, Rafiq created a checklist of the leadership actions to take to ensure he stayed focused on these influencing tips. He included a reminder to offer a couple of small choices in each meeting, as he could see how this helped to build a sense of connection with the team. He imagined that when bigger, more important decisions needed to be made, he would have a lot more goodwill to work with.

Even after decisions are made, there is value in continuing to remind people of the choices they made, to reinforce their sense of control. Remove choice and people feel coerced: you create anger, frustration and resistance. Provide choice and people feel a sense of influence over their world.

5. Now share facts

With a warm connection and a sense of agency, people are much more open to hearing new facts. Even at this point, though, it's not just about the facts. One of the most powerful ways to engage people to listen to new information and different viewpoints is to harness their curiosity. And what are people most curious about? What it means for them.

People want to know about themselves, and a positive message induces hope, not dread.

If you need to let someone know that their report was unsatisfactory, state that very clearly. Then highlight exactly what needs to be corrected, and what the reward – the future state – will be when it is corrected. Avoid focusing on what the consequences will be if the report is not made satisfactory. Hope comes from knowing what it is you need to do to get the reward: 'If I make the corrections to the report, I will know I have done a good job'.

What's your style?

To recap, warmth reflects the striving for union and solidarity. Its primary focus is on affiliation and relationship with others. Its opposite, coolness, reflects a greater formality in style and less focus on relationship.

Competence is task-focused and reflects dominance, or agency – the striving for control, power and mastery. The opposite is deference, or submission, which entails giving up your power to others.

These two dimensions – warm to cool and competent to deferent – form the basis[84] for eight different influencing styles:

1. Inspirer
2. Collaborator
3. Consulter
4. Appealer

5. Messenger
6. Legitimiser
7. Controller
8. Persuader.

Figure 7 overleaf depicts these eight styles and their relationship to the two key dimensions of warmth and competence.

According to emotional intelligence expert Daniel Goleman, 'executives must play their leadership styles like a pro – using the right one at the right time in the right measure. The payoff is in the results'.[85] Let's examine each style in turn.

Figure 7: What's your leadership influencing style?

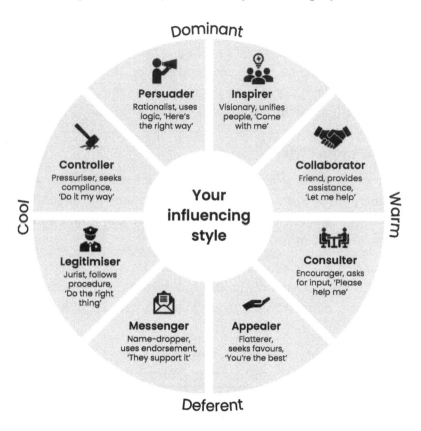

Dominant

Persuader
Rationalist, uses logic, 'Here's the right way'

Inspirer
Visionary, unifies people, 'Come with me'

Controller
Pressuriser, seeks compliance, 'Do it my way'

Collaborator
Friend, provides assistance, 'Let me help'

Your influencing style

Cool

Warm

Legitimiser
Jurist, follows procedure, 'Do the right thing'

Consulter
Encourager, asks for input, 'Please help me'

Messenger
Name-dropper, uses endorsement, 'They support it'

Appealer
Flatterer, seeks favours, 'You're the best'

Deferent

Inspirers

Of all leadership styles, Inspirer has the greatest positive impact on organisational climate.[86] Inspirers influence using dominance combined with warmth. They focus on creating a vision of what could be achieved, which creates excitement and anticipation – the key message is 'Come with me'. The basis of the Inspirer style is the 'clicking' that comes from connection. Painting a picture of a highly desirable future state gives meaning to shared work.

Collaborators

Collaborators influence using warmth and dominance. They focus on being friendly and engaging with others, and influence through assisting. The friendliness deepens relationships; it's warm because it is focused on what the other person needs. It is slightly dominant as it is focused on achieving your goals. The key message is 'Let me help'. This style also has an overall positive impact on organisational culture.

Consulters

Consulters influence using warm deference. They encourage others to provide their input and to make suggestions as well as express any concerns. They are open to improving their decisions based on the help they receive. The style is warm as it is based on helpfulness, and it is deferent as decisions are adjusted based on the help received. The message is 'Please help me'.

Appealers

Appealers influence using deference and warmth. They focus on ingratiating themselves to others, using their friendship as the basis for their influence. The style is deferent as it relies on flattery, and is warm because it uses personal favours to get results. Its key message is 'You're the best'.

Messengers

Messengers influence using cool deference. Their style is to gain support by associating with authority figures and supporters – they use the others' names and support to gain buy-in. The messenger style is cool because it relies on an implied association, and it is deferent as it places the decision power in the hands of others. The message is 'They support it'.

Legitimisers

Legitimisers influence using cool deference. They focus on using the rules and correct procedures to verify that something is the right thing to do. In other words, the rules provide a boundary within which an action is appropriate. The style is formal because it is rational rather than emotional, and it is submissive as it relies on rules set by others. 'It's the right thing to do.'

Controllers

Controllers influence using cool dominance, and focus on using their authority to compel action from others. They decide what needs to be done and apply pressure on others to comply. This style is formal because compliance is expected, and dominant because the action is created by the influencer. 'Do it my way' is the main message.

Persuaders

Persuaders influence using dominance and coolness, and appeal to rational logic to influence decisions. The style is cool as it's based on logic, and dominant as it assumes the persuader knows the one best way to do it – 'Here's the right way'.

***

All styles have legitimacy, depending on the circumstances. The cool styles are less effective when overused, however. Too much of the Persuader and Controller approaches reduces the quality of work, clarity about what needs to be done, and commitment, because they remove agency and choice.

Generally, people have one or two default styles. The important questions are: Are you as influential as you want to be? How easily do you flex your influencing style? What's the impact of the styles you tend to rely on?

Rafiq, for example, realised that his ability to assess what was happening and what was going wrong was limited. He didn't have as much insight into the context as he thought he did. He switched from the Persuader to the Inspirer style, focusing on painting a positive vision of the future and encouraging the team to be a part of it. He also decided to be more vulnerable with his team leader and use the Collaborator style, letting her know that he was doing so. He used just a small amount of 'Appealer' too, to increase the warmth in their interactions.

In response, his team leader chose to switch from a defensive mode into Consulter style with Rafiq, as well as to use that style more often with her team. The shift to a collaborative style between the two managers reassured the team and reduced their fear and concern. It also encouraged them to talk more openly about the team's issues.

Reading the context and selecting the right style is more effective than using the same style in each context.

For Rafiq, a key learning was to back his own judgement about how to approach the issue outlined by his boss. The need to flexibly adapt within his context and adopt the right influencing style for each person or group of people took some effort. However, it paid off quickly, and he was able to build on his new success. Rafiq's shift to the Inspirer and Collaborator styles gave the team hope and agency. They could articulate the issues they faced and choose what to do.

Flex your style to influence remotely

Staying influential feels a little trickier with remote work. However, bear in mind that it's not about the sheer number of interactions you have, it's how you engage with others that matters.

Focusing on warmth and relationship via remote methods is more difficult. Emotions are a little harder to read, and it can be harder to have ad hoc and less formal interactions. Don't rely just on videoconferencing for your interactions: it's easier to mask emotions during a video call and to merely pretend to attend. Phone calls, using voice only, provide more emotional information, so make sure you use them as part of your arsenal to convey warmth. Check back to Chapter 4 for more on connecting with your team remotely.

RESET YOUR STYLE

Don't try harder when you want to influence others – use a lighter touch to be more effective. Whether you're working remotely or not, matching your influencing style to your team and your circumstances is the key to having your biggest impact.

In summary, use these six steps to influence others to do what you want them to do:

1. Choose your influencing style/s. What does the context, rather than your ego, require?

2. Be warm. Show you care.

3. Suspend your ego. Connect with others to understand their needs.

4. Avoid inducing fear and stay positive. It's more pleasant for you and them.

5. Increase people's agency – offer them choice to enrol commitment.

6. Create a sense of realistic hope. Identify positive future benefits.

CHAPTER 8

FLEX YOUR DELEGATION

'If you want to do a few small things right, do them yourself.
If you want to do great things and make a big impact,
learn to delegate.' — John C. Maxwell[87]

Bill was experiencing yet another surge in his workload. While two of his five team leaders were performing well, it was a burden filling the gaps for the one who was underperforming and two who were new. Something had to give, and it felt like it was him.

Bill had experienced similar workload issues at times in the past; usually, he just kept pushing through until his colleagues were up to speed. But this could take three to nine months, and in the case of underperformers, occasionally things got worse rather than better.

Bill knew he needed to delegate more to the high performers and as part of the onboarding process for his new leaders. This would relieve some pressure and give him more time to devote to work on the underperformance issue. He struggled with delegation, however, largely due to his need for achievement and the standards he set. He needed to think differently to mobilise the full talent in his team if he was going to succeed.

The biggest impediment to flexAbility is not delegating enough. Delegating well is the most important thing you need to do to increase your flexAbility. When you delegate more work to more team members, you will achieve more by doing less.

This chapter introduces a framework for delegation that helps you to promote as much autonomy as possible. To delegate well, you need to invest time in building connection, trust, motivation, growth and autonomy. You do that by setting up psychological safety, coaching, recognising progress and offering feedback. The more time you invest in these activities, the bigger your payback, because you'll have a team bursting with talent and initiative and not afraid to use them!

Assess your delegation

Get started by identifying how you delegate at present and the risks and opportunities of increased delegation:

1. How clear and simple is your process for delegating?
2. What is your biggest barrier to delegating more?
3. What are the risks of delegating more? And of *not* delegating more?
4. What opportunity do you believe you have to delegate more?
5. What would be the ideal amount of delegation to free up your time?

Why delegating starts with psychological safety

The delegation framework, outlined below in Figure 8, starts with safety. Over the last few years we have become much more aware of the importance of psychological safety at work. It helps meet people's identity needs, and to feel comfortable to be themselves and use their full capabilities. Safety increases people's connection to each other and to work. The job of the leader is to set up relationships and teamwork for safety and connection.

Figure 8: Framework for increasing impact through delegation

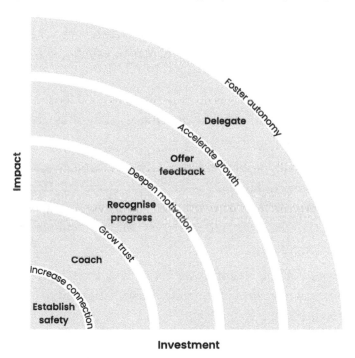

A climate of safety supports a focus on coaching as a primary means of engaging with the team. This grows trust. In the context of trusting relationships, it's both easier and more impactful to provide recognition to others for their work, which is the third layer in the diagram. Recognition for good work is the most motivating tool in a leader's toolkit – it helps people know that you appreciate the progress they contribute to and encourages more progress.

When people feel a sense of safety, trust and progress, they welcome feedback (the fourth layer). And offering feedback that shapes their skills and careers helps to accelerate their growth. As humans, we are never not growing: it's hardwired into us. Across history, humans have explored, grown, adapted and progressed. Unfortunately, many organisations and leaders suppress people's natural desire to learn and grow. When competition and compliance are the priorities, it's harder to explore and experiment – people become more cautious.

But you can harness the hardwiring by using good feedback, and make growth intentional and directional, as well as accelerate its pace.

Lack of autonomy is one of the social triggers that increases threat and contributes to burnout, as we saw in Chapter 1. Delegation is the last layer in the framework; the more that you can delegate to your team, the more autonomy they will feel, and the greater their satisfaction.

In the rest of this chapter, we'll examine each layer of the framework in more detail to provide you with the tools to improve how you delegate.

Establish safety to increase connection

You don't just need talent and capability in an organisation – you also need people to contribute their best ideas. And people need to feel psychologically safe to share information and report mistakes. When they feel safe, they feel connected and will take risks and be vulnerable.

According to Harvard leadership expert Amy Edmondson, a climate of psychological safety is one in which people feel able to express and be themselves. One where:

- skills and talents are valued and used
- efforts are not undermined
- you can ask others for help
- it's safe to take a risk
- being different is accepted
- you can bring up problems and issues
- mistakes are not held against you.[88]

For Bill, the onboarding of his new team leaders was an opportune time to review and increase the team's sense of safety. To set up for safety, he needed to do three things:

1. set expectations about safety
2. provide ways for everyone to contribute
3. respond to contributions.

1. Set expectations

Setting expectations helps the team to understand why psychological safety is important and how it works. What expectations do you have of each other? What will it mean to work together to ensure a safe climate for teamwork?

Discuss the value of sharing ideas and suggestions openly, and how doing so will make a positive contribution to the team's work. Discuss the value of identifying small errors and mistakes, too, and how this makes work easier and more enjoyable for everyone. Encourage people to see the value in voicing doubts and uncertainties.

One way to set expectations is to create some ground rules or a team charter to guide conversations. Examples of ground rules include keeping personal information confidential, identifying how you will raise differences of opinion, and beginning meetings with a check-in from each person. A set of ground rules provides a charter for how the team works together. A charter makes expectations explicit and ensures that team members are aware of what needs to be done and how to do it. (See also the discussion on team norms in Chapter 4, which provides suggestions about ground rules and the elements that you can include in a team charter.)

2. Invite participation

Once expectations have been set, people need to know how to contribute. As the leader, you need to build their confidence that their voice is welcome. Structures for getting input might include special meetings, items on existing meeting agendas, chat areas in your intranet and suggestion walls. You don't need special structures for seeking input, but you do need to signal where and how people can contribute their ideas – and then leave space for them to do so.

You can show that you don't have all the answers, acknowledge the gaps in your knowledge and ask for suggestions. Ask questions, even if you have the answers, and then listen. Offer help. Share tips on how you do things, how you learn and how you deal with uncertainty.

3. Respond productively

Acknowledge people's contributions. Even if you don't agree or won't implement every suggestion raised, thank people for their input. The focus isn't on doing everything that everyone suggests but on continuous learning. Your appreciation will go a long way: use it regularly.

Make it clear that mistakes will be accepted and that reasonable failures will be tolerated. Learning can't happen without error. What's important is to be able to notice an error early, to investigate why it occurred and then to take corrective action. Reskill, change the resourcing, stop doing some things and start others. Offer to help. The smaller the mistake or error, the more agile and responsive the team can be to fix it and learn from it.

In addition, when there are violations of safety – for example, when someone raises a problem and they are ignored – timely sanctions are necessary. You need to call out each violation and address it – and through whatever action you take, make sure people understand that it's not acceptable. Call out what's positive too, of course: that's even more motivating.

How to make it easier for everyone to say what they think

These are the things that everyone can do to help build psychological safety:

- Maintain eye contact in team discussion (keep your video on in Zoom).
- Engage in short, energetic exchanges.
- Don't interrupt.
- Ask lots of questions.
- Listen intently and show you've heard what's been said.
- Use humour and laughter.
- Say thank you for big and small things.
- Pay attention to building a sense of belonging.
- Take turns: give everyone a go.
- Work on hard problems as well as easy ones.
- Encourage candour.
- Keep reminding each other that this is a safe place to be open and honest.

> **Teams don't achieve great results because of how smart members are, but because of how safe the team climate is.**

Increasing psychological safety allows people's talents and perspectives to shine more brightly. It connects people to each other, allowing team members to solve shared problems and reducing turf wars. And all of this frees up your time.

Coach to grow trust

As a leadership style, coaching promotes a high level of trust. Building on the connections between you and your team, coaching helps them to learn and to achieve their highest aspirations. Coaching helps you to increase the warm leadership styles introduced in Chapter 7.

Coaching shows that you care, that you are committed to developing others, that you are sensitive to their needs and that you have a high positive regard for them. When you coach, you facilitate self-discovery and purposeful action; the result is that people feel capable and confident to do what you ask them to do and know that you support them.

The best way to help others grow and change is to coach them to move closer to their ideal selves.[89] Do this by spending the first 30 minutes of a coaching conversation focusing on their purpose or dreams for the future. Use the process from Chapter 2 that you used to work out your own purpose and aspiration. Help others to identify their ideal selves and clarify what is most meaningful to them.

It's critical not to overemphasise problems when you're coaching – even when there is a problem that needs to be solved. If you focus on the problematic behaviour without first focusing on the aspiration, there's only a 5 per cent chance that the behaviour will change. That's a *95 per cent* chance it won't! So, don't dive straight into the problem.

Bill's tendency was to do that with his underperforming team leader. While he tried to manage himself to be positive, his frustration with her inability to 'get it' meant that he was engaging without compassion. He needed to rise above that, be more empathetic and incorporate a focus on her ideal self. When he stopped focusing on the problem and started emphasising an ideal future, her trust in him increased.

As a result, their conversations became more open and less stilted. She envisioned her ideal self doing different kinds of work. She acknowledged that her interest in changing her career, as well as issues at home, had created friction that was distracting her from her work. Being permitted to explore this, and feeling supported in doing so, relieved some of the pressure and helped her refocus her attention on her work. Bill committed to coaching her in skills that would assist her to achieve her future aspiration, as well as in the current realities.

Being told we need to change is not an effective way to create and sustain behavioural change. Change takes effort – you must make it worth it. When it focuses on aspiration and possibility, coaching inspires a sense of hope – a feeling that 'It is possible for me to do this'.

As a leader who coaches, you can have the greatest influence on others by being a source of inspiration.

Show genuine caring, provide support and encouragement, and facilitate the discovery of your team members' 'ideal self'. People draw energy from their vision and will continue to put effort into growing, even when times are tough. They will also feel less stressed, experience greater renewal and keep learning and growing – as will you.

To coach well, you need to have the intention to coach, take the time to prepare for coaching conversations, and keep practicing.

Recognise progress to deepen motivation

Intrinsic motivation is the drive to do something because it's interesting, enjoyable or challenging. It's internally rewarding. The more that team members have intrinsic motivation for their work, the more work they will do, the better they'll do it and the more they'll enjoy it.

The simplest and yet most powerful tactic to increase intrinsic motivation is to recognise people's progress. Taking small daily opportunities to signal progress, such as noticing small wins, celebrating breakthroughs and noticing any kind of forward movement, as well as celebrating goal completion, significantly increases motivation. As leadership and motivation researchers Teresa Amabile and Steven Kramer put it, 'Small positive and negative events are tiny booster shots of psychological uppers and downers. In managing people, you really do have to sweat the small stuff'.[90]

It's a simple formula: the more positive you are about the work that's done, the more motivated you are and the more favourably you approach your work. The more that things get in your way at work, by contrast, the more negative you feel and the less motivated you are.

For example, a project team of three people may learn that their project is going on hold. One person interprets this as 'another' instance of management incompetence; they feel frustrated. A second person makes sense of it as creating a break for them:

'Great, I get a breather. I can stop working so hard.' They feel relief. A third person makes sense of it in a completely different way. They think it signals that there is something wrong with the work – 'It must be terrible', otherwise the project wouldn't have stalled. They feel dejected.

You can see how much interpretations can vary from person to person. With a good understanding of each person, however, you can coach to their individual needs and responses.

People's thoughts and feelings – frustration, relief or dejection – affect their desire to do the work: what they'll do, how they'll do it and when. There are many ways that you can support people to make positive sense of their work. You can influence motivation by noticing how you talk about what's happening, framing why events are taking place the way they are and clarifying what the organisation expects. How do you help people to see the positive and constructive in events? How do you manage your own response to setbacks and help both yourself and your team to recover as quickly as possible?

Again, the best way to help people increase their motivation is to recognise progress each day. What did we do today to make progress, to move forward with our work, to achieve our goals? It's also important to identify what gets in the way of progress, so people can recover from setbacks and remove hindrances and barriers. What do we need to do tomorrow to continue to make progress? As coach, notice progress and help your people reorient themselves around what worked and what needs to change.

When you notice progress, you recognise people's efforts and accomplishments. Increasing intrinsic motivation is where your leverage is.

Offer feedback to accelerate growth

In a context in which people feel safe and connected, trust you and are intrinsically motivated, you can accelerate their growth by offering feedback. The more supportive your relationship is with your team members, the easier it will be for them to listen to and welcome your feedback. If they know you value them, they'll care about what you think of them and welcome your opinion on how they can grow and improve.

Feedback is much maligned and often avoided. When we hear that someone is going to 'give feedback', the assumption is that it will be negative. That's unhelpful, because people want feedback – yes, they do! Top performers say they want feedback to grow, but only about half of them get what they need, according to Therese Huston.[91] Gen Z want regular feedback that focuses on growing their skills. So, it isn't that people don't want feedback, it's that they don't want *bad* feedback; unsurprisingly, most people will avoid feeling crushed if they can!

It isn't that people aren't prepared to accept tough feedback, though; it's how it's given that matters. There's a huge penalty for sloppy feedback: 80 per cent of people who receive feedback that is demotivating start to look for other jobs.

All it takes is a split second

Here's food for thought: even if you don't realise it, you're always giving feedback. Feedback is occurring constantly, in micro-moments, often non-verbally, frequently unintentionally.

Feedback occurs in a split second and is automatic. Whether you make eye contact with someone, whether you show that you're listening to what they say, whether you ask them a follow-up question, the amount of time you spend with them – these are all pieces of feedback. Employees are constantly evaluating whether they matter, whether you recognise their skills, and whether they've said or done the right thing.

What you convey in these subtle ways may or may not be consistent with the feedback that you *want* to give. There is terrific value in becoming more congruent and intentional when you give feedback. When you give regular feedback that comes from a genuine desire to be of service, and the feedback is aligned with the person's ideal self, it becomes generative. When you prepare for and practise giving feedback, it becomes more intuitive, then drops in to become part of your routine interactions with your team. It feels easier and is more rewarding for both them and you.

Feedback is scary when it evokes social threat

In Chapter 1, I shared the way the autonomic nervous system works, and David Rock's social threat triggers. As a quick reminder, when we feel threatened we shut down, we don't listen, we can't process information and won't act on it. We become defensive and self-protective. Feedback may well evoke such a sense of threat.

You can reduce the threat response by preparing your feedback so that it meets people's needs. People want the feedback they're given to:

- acknowledge their hard work
- be accurate and specific
- include a chance to discuss the feedback and to say what they think of it
- be two-way – they want to be listened to by the feedback giver
- identify what needs to happen next and what's expected in the future

- come after advance warning, so that they know they're going to receive it
- be given by someone they trust.[92]

If you want people to take on board your feedback, they need to hear you – and their threat response needs to be minimised so that they can.

One of the key points in the list above is that people want feedback to be a two-way process. The best way to activate someone's interest in listening to what you have to say is to show your willingness to listen to them. That's why feedback is the fourth step in the delegation framework. 'I know you care about me and my growth, and so I value your feedback, even if it's tough to hear.'

Creating a climate in which people ask for feedback will also give them a greater sense of control over it. You can start by role-modelling this: ask for feedback from your team and show them how to provide it. It's best to ask for feedback immediately after an action or event, as this increases the opportunity to be specific and accurate. It also provides the opportunity to act on the feedback quickly.

For example, you could say, 'I'd like some feedback on the meeting we just had'. Identify what you want to know about: perhaps, 'I'd like your views on how clearly I communicate with the team, and whether people know what they need to do after our meetings. What do I need to improve so that the team is clear about the next steps?'

Ask broadly: get feedback from a range of stakeholders to mitigate unconscious bias in any one feedback giver.

The way that you receive your feedback is another important aspect of role-modelling. If someone says they'd like to give you feedback, but now isn't a good time, say so, and schedule a time later in the day or the next. Then listen. Don't interrupt, become defensive or try to explain your behaviour. Allow yourself to pause, reflect and ask for clarification if you need it. Ask for suggestions about what to do differently. And say thank you.

Suggest a timeframe in which you'll get back to the person for follow-up; this should be after you've had time to make changes. That way, you're signalling that you have taken the feedback seriously and have every intention of acting on it.

Use the same approach with team members if they ask you for feedback: let them know you are happy to do so. Ask what feedback would be most helpful to them right now, listen to their response and then provide feedback consistent with their request. You want to create a climate in which people readily admit they need help or don't know what to do; attuning your feedback to their identified needs will help to do that.

To give feedback, start with an affirmation to signal your positive intent. 'I really want good things for you.' Lead with praise: recognise their recent good work and how much value it provides. Examples include when they've gone above and beyond, been proactive and taken initiative, taken responsibility for a problem or neglected need, offered good ideas, showed loyalty and commitment or promoted teamwork. Focus on something, anything you can, that has improved. Even if the person's performance isn't that great, don't skimp on the praise – but make sure it's genuine.

Have a growth mindset – let the person know that you believe they can change and improve. Also, hook them into past successes, reminding them of when they successfully undertook the behaviour or changed other behaviour in the past. 'How could you do this more often?'

Asking questions is a great way to deepen your feedback. 'What other ways might you do x?'; 'I've noticed a few occasions, a and b for example, when z happened – what are your observations about why that happened?'

When you've discussed the feedback and future options, have the person state their takeaways to ensure a shared understanding.

Setting up a pattern of mutual feedback-giving helps everyone to lift their game.

It might be counter-intuitive, but giving remote feedback via phone is more effective than via videoconference.[93] Facial cues can be easily masked over VC, and so it can be hard to get an accurate read on how the person is responding to your feedback. With only auditory cues to attend to by phone, you are better able to tune into someone's emotional state. Also, we think more freely without visual cues and brainstorm better options, so discussion by phone can be much more fruitful.

Here are a few tips on what to avoid when you are giving feedback. Don't:

- back out or make excuses for the person
- pull in your own experiences
- say that you used to have the same problem
- cushion your feedback ('You're not going to like hearing this')
- label the feedback ('I have some negative feedback to give you')
- be insensitive ('You were a real windbag')
- give advice ('Let me tell you what you need to do')
- make it about the person ('You were disruptive today') – instead, make it about their behaviour
- delay the feedback ('Last month...').[94]

Feedback accelerates growth. The greater the safety, trust and motivation you create, the more discomfort will be tolerated, and greater growth will be the result. As a flexAble leader, you are highly motivated to accelerate the growth, skills and capabilities of your team. The more capable they are, and the more confident they are that you trust them, the more you can delegate to them.

INSIGHT

Trust and growth make delegation easier

Chapter 1 explored the working of the autonomic nervous system and the role of the parasympathetic nervous system (PNS) in triggering rest-and-digest, the state that allows renewal. As we've discussed, the kinds of questions that leaders ask can trigger either fight-or-flight or rest-and-digest modes. A lack of safety, asking the wrong kinds of questions, not recognising people's contributions or providing feedback badly can all trigger fight-or-flight. As fight-or-flight mode induces fear and anxiety, people will respond defensively to protect themselves from these unpleasant thoughts and feelings.

By contrast, creating a safe atmosphere, creating connection and trust, asking questions about someone's ideal or aspirational self and showing you care all trigger the PNS. This evokes awe, joy, gratitude and curiosity – and fMRI studies show that spending 30 minutes in this kind of conversation activates more PNS activity. The PNS then stimulates the vagus nerve and vasodilators, which increase blood flow, making you feel warmer. Blood pressure and pulse rates drop. Breathing slows and deepens.

We need the sympathetic nervous system (SNS) response to survive in physically threatening situations. We also need it to help us perform tasks quickly; a burst of adrenaline increases performance and stimulates rapid responses. Yet in our crazy, busy, overworked world, we are too often in fight-or-flight mode. A continual focus on meeting targets, problem-solving and analytics keeps the SNS activated.

Safety, trust, coaching, recognition and autonomy evoke rest-and-digest mode. They act as tipping points to help people intentionally change. When the specific changes you want to make are wrapped in the reason for making them, you are much more likely to succeed. You and your team can be vigilant to ensure that you are working to the right balance of performance and renewal.

Delegate to foster autonomy

Delegating helps to rebalance the amount of time leaders devote to work of low versus high risk or importance. Too many low-risk decisions are made at senior levels, which reduces the focus on strategy and oversight. Many of the leadership challenges profiled in this book highlight this problem.

When deciding what to delegate, a key consideration is the level of risk involved in the decision. That helps you decide who needs to be involved, how much time to spend on it, how much certainty is required and what your tolerance is for error.

A 70 per cent rule can help increase your tolerance for error. Can someone else perform the task at least 70 per cent as well as you can? If so, then you should delegate it. It might be frustrating that the task isn't done to your quality standard. To address this, plan to consistently increase people's capabilities so that they move from 70 per cent to 100 per cent. They can only do that, of course, when they do the tasks and get helpful feedback. The extra upside of allowing people to take on more tasks is that they may discover new and better ways to do them.

As the leader, delegate as much as you can and retain only the high-risk, critical business decisions.

A sliding scale of delegation

Rather than thinking of delegation as binary – either you do or you don't – consider what it might look like on a sliding scale.[95] As people's skills and confidence grow, delegate more responsibility to them.

Bill introduced a five-level sliding scale of delegation to help free up time and to show his trust in his team. He began by mapping what the five levels meant for their work, and shared this with his team. Involving them ensured shared understanding, allowed improvements to be identified and led to strong commitment from the team. Simply having the conversation felt empowering to them.

On the sliding scale, level 1 has the lowest level of authority and level 5 has the greatest autonomy to make decisions and take actions:

- **Level 1** – the person assesses the issue, explains to you what they've learned about it and identifies what options they would recommend. Encourage them to identify many options and review their strengths and weaknesses. You then make the decision, explaining why you chose the option you did.

- **Level 2** – the person assesses the issue, identifies options and then makes a recommendation about what to do. You retain the decision-making power, reserving the right to approve or amend the recommended course of action.

- **Level 3** – the person makes a recommendation. If they don't hear back from you within, say, 24 hours of you receiving the recommendation, they can proceed with it.

- **Level 4** – the person assesses the options, takes their preferred course of action and informs you of the action and its outcomes. You are no longer approving decisions but being informed about them.

- **Level 5** – this is full delegation. The person takes care of the decision and action using their own approach, and without reporting back to you.

Over time, your expectation should be that decisions will be delegated at increasingly higher levels.

Note that you should apply the levels to tasks, not to people. The same person might have tasks at different levels of delegation, due to the risk associated with each decision and the person's strengths and experiences. As new tasks and decisions arise, the level of delegation for each one is agreed. Issues that arise can be treated as coaching moments, to clarify and confirm approval and autonomy boundaries, and to pinpoint opportunities for further development.

The sliding scale is a powerful guide to help people build their skills. For some, it may offer a helpful reality check if their ambition is out of balance with their skills and they want more autonomy than you are prepared to give them. In any case, it provides a simple, effective basis for shared understanding of expectations and autonomy levels.

RESET YOUR DELEGATION

Delegation is perhaps the most powerful weapon for increasing your flexAbility. Workloads won't get lighter, the demands you face aren't going to ease – and as a high achiever, you're going to maintain your standards. The way to avoid overwork and burnout and to have greater freedom is to delegate routinely and rigorously.

Grant yourself greater freedom and enjoyment by resetting your delegation using the five-step framework we've discussed:

1. Establish a climate of safety to increase connection.

2. Increase the amount of time you spend coaching, to grow trust.

3. Recognise progress, as this will deepen people's intrinsic motivation.

4. Within trusting relationships, offer feedback to accelerate the growth of your team.

5. Use a clear framework for delegating and team members' autonomy and accountability will increase.

CHAPTER 9

FLEX YOUR IMPACT

'When you want to motivate, persuade, or be remembered,
start with a story of human struggle and eventual triumph.
It will capture people's hearts — by first attracting their brains.'
— Paul Zak[96]

Avery was a much more impactful leader than she gave herself credit for. The feedback from her bosses, peers and colleagues was glowing — her teams loved working with her, her colleagues appreciated her collaboration and support, and her boss congratulated her for always going above and beyond. From time to time, however, they expressed their concern about just how hard she worked.

Avery recognised that at times she could be her own worst enemy. Sure, there was a culture of overwork, and there was always more to do than it was possible to do. No matter how hard she worked, she wasn't going to change that.

So, it was time to challenge both herself and the system. To do that, Avery realised that she needed a new storyline for herself, one that reflected her flexAble purpose. She said she wanted balance in her life, yet she usually worked 55 to 60 hours a week. That created confusion. She needed a way to communicate her intentions clearly and make it easier to both gain the support of her stakeholders and increase her impact.

As a high-achieving, conscientious and agreeable leader, Avery had been sucked into the slipstream of overworking. It was hard to break free of this slipstream – it had a seduction and ease all of its own, pulling her along without making her think about where she was going or why. She'd lived the pain of that for too long!

With leaders around you – some creating the slipstream and others, like you, caught up in it – you've got to find a way to break free. When you articulate your why and what for leading flexAbly, you can create your own flow to lift you up and carry you along in your chosen direction.

In this chapter, we bring it all together. I'll show you how to script your compelling flexAbility story, which will help you to find clarity. It will also help you to increase your conviction in your flexAbility path: what you say yes or no to.

When you're clear about your story, you will convey it with presence. Story doesn't just help others make sense of you and understand who you are, it creates rapport and empathetic connection: it appeals to others. When your communication is targeted and authentic and you express yourself with conviction, you create an emotional resonance with others. Stories help you boost this resonance, and with it your impact.

Having clarified your purpose in Chapter 2, set up your work structure and routines to help you do what matters in Part II, and broadened your ability to influence and delegate in Chapters 7 and 8, you're ready to create your new compelling story, with flexAbility at its heart.

Assess your impact

Here's the final assessment to help you increase your flexAbility. Consider your impact and how you might improve it:

1. How clearly do you communicate your flexAble purpose?
2. How well do others understand what you stand for?
3. How comfortable are you with using your own story or stories when you communicate with others, both what you say and how you say it?
4. How would you like to improve your presence?
5. How well do your existing stories resonate with others?

Figure 9 provides an illustration of the framework for this chapter. It starts with story; the clearer and more authentic your storyline, the more compelling it is. Without a clear story, there is a gap, an absence. In that space, people might invent their own stories about you, if they care enough. Are these the stories you want them to tell? Probably not, if they don't fully know what you stand for.

Prepare and script the key stories that convey your flexAbility and your leadership essence. There's an easy process for creating and polishing your stories that I'll walk you through in the next section of this chapter. Your stories will be crystal clear. You will know what you stand for and so will others; stories make it easy for others to know what's important to you.

The way you tell your stories also matters. Once you have a clear script, you can share your stories powerfully and with presence. 'Presence' is the ability to project a sense of ease, authenticity and poise when you communicate with others.

Compelling story arcs, combined with your presence, will help to increase emotional connection so that you create a sense of resonance with others. Resonance is an amplification of your presence, a sense of shared connection and identification with others. Others will care about you, support you and advocate for you. They'll believe in you.

Figure 9: Increase your impact through narrative and presence

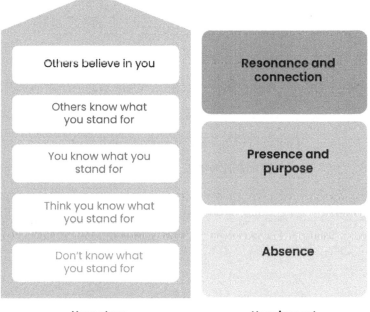

Crafting purposeful stories allows you to bring together your work from the previous chapters, map it into a succinct storyline, and then use it to infuse your communication with more meaning and value. The clearer you are about how flexAbility powers your leadership, the better you can communicate it.

Script your compelling stories

Stories are a great way to attract and hold attention, and as we've seen earlier in the book, attention is an important currency of leadership. You need people to pay attention to you if you are going to have impact. According to neuroeconomist Paul Zak, stories do more than attract and hold attention, however: they also change others' attitudes, beliefs and behaviours.[97]

Information conveyed through story is up to 20 per cent more memorable. People more easily recall a story and its associated feelings than other kinds of information.

INSIGHT

Stories create connection, resonance, commitment and impact

Character-driven storytelling has the power to substantially increase the release of oxytocin. Oxytocin increases feelings of empathy, which in turn increases rapport – it increases our connection to others. We are more likely to understand others and know how they will react. The amount of oxytocin that is released is predictive of how much people are willing to help others.

Experiments show that having a sense of higher purpose also stimulates oxytocin production, as does trust. Oxytocin is a key neurological signal for trustworthiness. And people will trust you more if you trust them first. Through the decision to trust them, you create a burst of oxytocin for yourself. Following the burst, you have 30 minutes in which the oxytocin heightens empathy in you. The empathy you display creates a reciprocal response in them – they will trust you to the same extent that you trust them.

Trust and purpose then mutually reinforce each other, providing a mechanism for extended oxytocin release, which increases happiness.

Note that, while oxytocin turns on when we are shown trust, it shuts down in environments of high stress or high competition.[98] If you trust others, by contrast, you set up a virtuous cycle of trust, empathy, connection and inspiration.

How stories work

Stories that involve human struggle, that develop and triumphantly resolve tension, create the most attention. Listeners come to share the emotions of the story protagonist and will mimic their feelings and behaviours. If you communicate your purpose through your story, people will empathise with you, feel the tension of your struggle and take pleasure in its resolution. This is why 'origin' stories, 'overcoming the monster' and 'rags to riches' stories are all so powerful.

A story guides people to know why they should care about you, and about what you are asking them to do. How will they feel when they're with you, or when you ask something of them?

At this point you may be thinking to yourself, 'But I'm not a "natural" storyteller'. Or you may think that you don't have a story that's interesting enough to engage people. Neither are true. We are all hardwired to tell and respond to stories, and we tell stories more than we notice. We're not always mindful about the messages we convey, though, given the speed of activity around us. We sometimes respond in staccato dot points and brief facts to 'get to the point' quickly.

Humble leaders may feel some discomfort about storytelling, too, as they don't want to 'blow their own horn'. The idea of storytelling may seem too self-aggrandising. However, the stories you create will not be like that at all. You won't just retain your humility: your stories will be a vehicle to convey it.

Some may think that creating stories seems a little false. However, what you're doing is taking the time to craft authentic stories so that your communication is better aligned with what you value most. You're always conveying messages: this is an opportunity to review them and recalibrate so that you're clear about what you stand for. Your stories make it easier to share who you truly are with others so that they come to understand what you stand for and can believe in you.

Script your story

Start by identifying some experiences that stand out to you. They might relate to your purpose, or to your goal to be more flexAble, or to how you want to increase your impact. They will be your own experiences.

You may well have stories about yourself that don't serve you well. Your inner critic will have some! This is a good time for rescripting, for focusing on what's positive and for projecting your best self and your aspirations.

So, brainstorm a list of relevant experiences. The kinds you might consider include:

- when you faced uncertainty and what you learned from it, or how you were able to create a sense of certainty and purpose
- a time when you felt challenged about the choices you were making
- an 'a-ha' moment – for example, when your purpose was clarified or confirmed, or you felt the value of making a choice that was aligned with your purpose

- a time when you persisted and made an impact using the motivation of your purpose
- a regret – a time when you were not living your values, and what the consequences were
- a turning point or crisis
- a time when you pursued a dream
- a situation when you faced a conflict between your purpose, goals, family and personal needs
- a time when you believed in yourself and achieved something against the odds.

Then, choose one to develop into your story:[99]

1. Write the point of your story in a single sentence. What's the message you want to convey?

2. Who is the audience for your story? Some stories may be suitable for any audience; some may be used with a range of different people but need tailoring for each group. Some may be appropriate for only one audience, such as your team.

3. Identify what you want them to feel – for example, motivated, compassionate, excited or in solidarity with you.

4. Then, take your story idea and plot it against a timeline. What happened first, next, and how did it end?

A good story needs a beginning, middle and end – that's what signals it as a story. It needs to be about a specific event that evokes a particular emotion. Script the story, paying attention to how you start, how you build momentum in the middle and how you end. The best stories are brief, so you're aiming for 60 to 90 seconds worth of story.

We are hardwired to tell and hear stories, and time and place signal the start of a story.

- **Start with a specific time and place** – use bullet points to keep your story brief and the pace lively. Use adjectives and adverbs to evoke emotions and the senses, as these will help the reader or listener experience your story at a more physical and emotional level. For example, 'It was two weeks into Melbourne's sixth pandemic lockdown, and rather than restrictions lifting, to my dismay, they were tightening even further. Yet again, we were going to have to delay the start of Project X. I felt overwhelmed by the number of delays, by the frustration of starting and restarting this project.'
- **Move to your middle** – frame your characters, make sure you keep it succinct and use graphic imagery wherever you can.
- **Make your ending clear and powerful** – the first kind of ending is a bridge ('I'm sharing this with you because…'). The second kind of ending is a link ('Imagine the impact if we…' or 'What I learned was…'). Then stop talking.

Sometimes it can be helpful to use present tense when you tell a story. This gives an air of immediacy; for example, 'It's 2008 and I'm standing in front of an angry group of customers'.

Here's an example story that focuses on purpose and flexAbility:

In June 2020, I was asked to step in and sort out a project being run by a colleague who's a well-known power-player. The project was way off track. Complaints were piling up. It was such a mess. I struggled to get on top of the complexity of it all; I was neglecting my regular work and not making headway on anything.

For six weeks, I hung on by my fingertips. I started to feel ground down, incompetent; I wondered what the hell I was trying to do. I pride myself on doing a good job and being

*available to help with tricky challenges like this. I know that I'm
good at it. But this one got me.*

*I hadn't realised how close to burnout I was before I was asked
to take the project on, and it was the straw that broke the
camel's back. I had to take three weeks' leave to recover.*

*This became a real turning point for me in my determination
to live my life on purpose and flexibly. What's most important
to me is that I influence transformational change across our
industry to deliver sustainable environmental outcomes and to
do what is necesssary to manage my commitments well.*

*If my normal is 'Everything anyone asks of me at any time',
I'm always going to be at the edge of burnout. That's why I now
manage my availability as closely as I do.*

Here's another example that focuses on leadership purpose:

*I felt like I was thrown in at the deep end in my first leadership
role. I'd applied for a position but was offered a different role,
two levels up. I felt totally out of my depth.*

*Less than a year later, I was asked to take on an even bigger
leadership role in the region, with responsibility for numerous
sites. I remember saying to my boss that I couldn't possibly do it:
I was still getting to grips with my existing leadership role. It felt
daunting to take on responsibility for so many other leaders
when I felt so green. Despite my reservations, though, I agreed
to do it for six months. I was convinced that I would want to go
back after that.*

*Six months later, I had no intention of going back. I got great
satisfaction from working with the leaders, helping them to bring
their teams up to speed and supporting them to really stretch
themselves. I 'knew my stuff': my experience was actually
helping them. And I wanted to keep doing it.*

I'm lucky that I've had several leaders in my career who have seen capability in me that I didn't see for myself, and who have encouraged me to step into new challenges. I hope that in each of my leadership roles, I've helped to do the same thing, to build the confidence of the leaders I've worked with: helped them to back themselves and believe in their ability to lead.

To create maximum impact, stories need to:

- have a clear point
- be brief – 60 to 90 seconds
- be congruent with your beliefs
- be real.

Practise, practise, practise

Once you've scripted your story or stories, start practising. Rehearse them, record yourself telling them, play them back to review how they sound, then edit. This also helps you learn the scripts so that you can deliver them naturally and authentically.

Try to get some specific feedback on each story, including the effect it has on your audience.

With this level of investment, it makes sense to repeat your stories. Some stories lend themselves to several different messages – you can use them in multiple ways, changing some of the lessons learned, or perhaps changing the ending and the bridge you use.

On the other hand, you may develop a story as a one-off – if, for example, you have a key presentation coming up and you want it to be memorable. Start with a story to create attention and to help highlight the most important point you want to make.

Your story should be designed to create an emotional connection with your audience. To give the story life, inject your emotion into it: relive it as you tell it.

Increase your presence

How you deliver your story, your expressiveness, makes all the difference. This is what presence is. Amy Cuddy defines presence as 'the state of being attuned to and able to comfortably express our true thoughts, feelings, values, and potential'.[100] Presence isn't something you do or don't have, it's something that you might or might not create in this moment.

Cuddy goes on to say:

> *'Presence emerges when we feel personally powerful, which allows us to be acutely attuned to our most sincere selves. In this psychological state, we are able to maintain presence even in the very stressful situations that typically make us feel distracted and powerless.'*

The model of influencing I introduced in Chapter 7 priori-tises warmth and connection. The same principle is at work here – showing warmth demonstrates trustworthiness and is the foundation of presence.

Presence experts Kathy Lubar and Belle Linda Halpern outline a simple four-step process for increasing your presence:[101]

1. Be present.
2. Reach out.
3. Be more expressive.
4. Stay congruent.

Each step has both an interior and an exterior aspect. The interior aspect concerns your state of mind and heart; your intention. The exterior aspect is the behaviour that reflects your intention: what it looks like to others.

1. Be present

Presence starts with being completely 'in the moment'. When the stakes are high – for example, if we're attempting to influence an authority figure – we may feel a sense of threat. Our sympathetic nervous system may kick in, and at worst, we may freeze, our minds going blank. Identity threat may interfere. We may not always feel that we get our message across, provide our best argument or work through all the points that we laboriously prepared.

Contrast these moments with those when you have felt present and in flow. It may have been in a work context, or when you were playing sport or lost in playing or listening to music. There was an intensity to your experience, right at that moment. When you are fully present, you are focused.

We are continually tested to remain present, so remind yourself of the suggestions for managing your attention. Use STOP, from Chapter 5. Or focus on your breath: consciously take four or five deep breaths in the belly and notice the calm it produces. When you begin to feel under pressure, focusing on the breath can help reduce anxiety, increase your calmness and allow you to better focus. By breathing through the belly, the fight-or-flight response can be inhibited and the PNS rest-and-digest mode activated.

When you are present, you can tune in to notice and listen.

2. Reach out

Reaching out is about building relationships through empathy and authentic connection. Being able to listen to others is critical to presence; it helps you to understand what makes others tick. The ability to link from their feelings and experiences back to your own helps to create connection. And as Lubar and Halpern say, 'The paradox of listening is that by relinquishing power – the temporary power of speaking, asserting, knowing – we become more powerful'.[102] (Note the resemblance to coaching.)

Here are the three things to do to reach out:

1. **Listen for the subtext, as well as the obvious** – what's really going on? The subtext is where people reveal their intentions and values. Listen for the links and connections. Listen for values and strengths.
2. **Acknowledge the person** – call out the strengths and values that you've recognised. Paraphrase what they've said, confirm the values and offer insights as they occur to you.
3. **Share yourself** – share your stories, values, strengths and concerns to build trust and awareness.

> **People want to know who you are, and they're looking for points of connection with you.**

3. Be more expressive

Expressiveness is the ability to express your feelings using words, voice, posture and face to deliver a congruent message. (Check back to Chapter 3 and the Wheel of Emotions.)

Every exchange you have is an opportunity to reveal your interests. What are you fighting for? What are the obstacles? What do others want? What will be most important to do? Use words that capture your purpose.

To increase your expressiveness, whether you are communicating with one person or a room full of people, try these three tactics:

1. **Use heightened language to increase interest.** Avoid boring, business-speak words like 'inform' and 'announce'. Try words that convey greater interest, like 'impress' and 'inspire'. Use words that are full of life. For example, rather

than focusing on 'debriefing' at the end of a difficult project, focus on 'celebrating achievements'. Conveying energy provokes interest and engagement. You can do that by imbuing what you say with appropriate and authentic feeling. If you express enthusiasm, you tend to evoke enthusiasm; but if you don't put emotional energy in, you're not likely to get any back. (Be careful, though, about how you communicate strong negative feelings.)

2. **Use vocal variety to avoid the monotone trap.** Vary your pitch using highs and lows, and add warmth to your voice. Use pauses; while we often think that pauses are bad, in fact the audience needs time to process what you're saying. A longer pause after an important point lends it weight. Try recording yourself in conversation to assess the variety of your pitch, tone, warmth and rhythm.

3. **Align your body language with your message.** Stay aware of your posture; stand tall. Use facial expressions and gestures to enliven your message. Use eye contact to connect with your audience.

In addition, to be most engaging as a storyteller, you need to be humble and appropriately vulnerable. If you use humour, it should only be self-deprecating; making jokes for effect, or at others' expense, will detract from your message.

4. Stay congruent

The simplest way to remain congruent with others is to be sincere. As you're learning new skills and tactics, you may feel uncomfortable and question how authentic you appear to be. A reasonable level of discomfort is a good indicator of learning, however, so keep practising. With practice, new scripts and increased expressiveness will feel natural. And if you mean what you say, even if you're not perfect at saying it yet, you're sincere.

The more that you accept yourself, the more authentic you will seem to others, and the more easily you will be able to reflect your FlexAbility in your decisions and actions.

The clarity you'll gain from the activities in this chapter will assist you to craft your leadership story. Exploring, creating and rehearsing your story helps create greater congruence and confidence. That helps you and others to change and grow. The easier it is for you to share your story with others, the easier it will be for them to recognise your leadership and appreciate your flexAbility.

Spark resonance

Presence is how you show up; resonance is how others connect with you. When you express your presence, you increase your connection with others. Stories about character – who you are – create empathy in others. When your story develops tension, it holds attention and the audience empathises with you. They feel what you feel, they trust you and will cooperate more readily with you.

Who you are resonates with who they are and is inspiring.

Resonance means that you fully engage yourself in service to those around you. Use the power of your stories to create contagious connections – to move and inspire people to work and be their best. You offer courage and hope that there is a future beyond overwork, one worth striving for.

RESET YOUR IMPACT

The biggest challenge to achieving your purpose and goals sustainably and enjoyably is the pressure to overwork. When you sacrifice too much of your life and your energy to the treadmill of overwork, you burn up, then burn out. But don't break down, give in or give up! Instead, use the power of your purpose to create stories that compel you and move others to create a human, flexAble working world that frees you from overwork to follow your dreams.

When you increase your flexAbility, you increase your impact. Stories are powerful tools for this. Decide what being flexAble means to you, then share it with others:

1. Script your story or stories about who you are as a leader and what being flexAble means to you.

2. Share your story with others.

3. Show up with presence as your authentic self.

4. Create resonance with others, and spark energy and commitment that helps everyone break free of overwork and live fulfilled lives.

AFTERWORD

It was impossible to imagine the profound impact COVID-19 would have on our lives. If there was a silver lining to the pandemic, however, it was that work practices would be fundamentally changed. After years of slow progress on making flexible work mainstream – placing trust in workers that they would get their work done wherever and whenever they worked – we looked set to take a quantum leap forward.

Early indications were that flexible, remote work was here to stay. While some parts of the economy have been ravaged by the pandemic, most have survived and some have thrived, and many have done so without workers needing to be in the office at all.

Now, a couple of years down the track, the 'great reset' remains a hope rather than a reality. But it has exposed two things:

1. The issue is not whether it's possible to work from home, it is *leaders' ability to trust* that the work will get done.
2. Work demands are relentlessly increasing; this is now so routine as to be rendered invisible.

For people to excel in such an environment, they are compelled to overwork.

It's the prevailing work culture of overpromising, long hours and presenteeism that fuels the need for people to make sacrifices and trade-offs – whether they be career-based, as was the case for

Avery; family-based, as was the case for Marco; or health-based, as is the case for many. And as we've seen from all the leaders profiled in this book, the pandemic seems to have made this even worse. Working more hours in an environment of heightened uncertainty and anxiety has exacted a hefty personal toll: burnout has doubled.

To focus on the core of the problem means that workload expectations must be addressed. Without this, chronic stress and burnout rates will continue to exact their heavy, and unnecessary, toll. Whether or not you're at a senior leadership level with the power to change the work demands and culture of your organisation, there are improvements you can make.

Chapter 1 outlined the serious consequences – including death – of the chronic stress and burnout that overwork causes. The chapter also outlined what can be done to make work less stressful. It offered a series of tactics that any leader can implement to improve the working lives of their teams and make a meaningful difference to their day-to-day experience. Manage your own workload, stress and burnout well, and be a beacon of hope for others, that they too can do the same.

Chapter 2 outlined how to reset your purpose. Purpose is both inspiring and a critical weapon for increasing your flexAbility. When you know why you do what you do, you can hold firm against the erosion of work into your life and your freedom. You can set and pay better attention to maintaining your boundaries.

Being psychologically flexible is another superpower for increasing your flexAbility, and its core features were discussed in Chapter 3. Staying focused on what matters most can be a challenge without it. Thinking mindfully, feeling freely and learning openly will stand you in good stead against the daily whirlwind of too many competing demands.

The focus of Part II was on how to do the work that matters most. Its three chapters focused in turn on structuring your work to be more efficient and effective by playing to your strengths (Chapter 4), making time for deep, focused work (Chapter 5), and making your work routine effortless by reviewing and adjusting your habits (Chapter 6). The chapters are full of tactics and techniques to help you adjust your working day and improve the working days of your colleagues, wherever you and they are.

Chapter 7 provides an antidote to the demanding styles of influencing that fuel overwork, showing you how to be more influential by starting with warmth and taking care to understand others' motivations. These styles, and the tactics introduced in Chapter 8, are all investments in trust and relationships, and they can help liberate you from overwork. Chapter 8 discusses how to establish the right kind of climate for delegation, and this is perhaps the most important chapter in the book: to prevent yourself from overworking you *must* delegate freely and rigorously. The more you can let it go and show your trust in others, the freer you can be.

Finally, in Chapter 9 the focus is on increasing your presence through mobilising and inspiring those around you while maintaining your own flexAble work practices. Create a wonderful, compelling story of your leadership flexAbility and inspire others to seek a healthy and successful life without overwork's sacrifices and trade-offs.

Being a high achiever who is conscientious and agreeable is the essence of your success. Organisations and colleagues love high performers like you: you are the ideal worker. You're switched on, hardworking and hold yourself to account – you're prepared to do what it takes.

But this is also what can trip you up. If you don't pay attention to your own needs and energy levels, you'll end up working too hard, trying too hard and caring too much. Time will feel like confetti, and despite working increasingly long hours to get it all done, you will feel unsatisfied. Chronic stress and burnout then loom, especially if you are particularly passionate about your work.

I've had the enormous privilege of coaching the high-achieving leaders profiled in the book – and many others like them – and know that our organisations are indeed in good hands. When you are at your energetic best, working flexAbly and being purposeful, focused and influential, you provide the blueprint for our future world of work. You are the reset we need.

'In a gentle way, you can shake the world.'
– Attributed to Mahatma Gandhi

Use this book for yourself and within your circle of influence to help reset the work experience of your colleagues and the culture of your team. Work your way through the resets in this book, identifying where you would gain the most benefit, aligning your actions with your purpose as you go. Free yourself to be flexAble, to know what matters, do what matters and influence what matters most.

REFERENCES

1   B Schulte, *Overwhelmed: Work, love, and play when no one has the time*, Pan Macmillan, USA, 2014.

2   World Economic Forum, *The Great Reset*, 19 July 2020, https://www.weforum.org/great-reset.

3   R Harfoush, *Hustle and Float: Reclaim your creativity and thrive in a world obsessed with work*, 1st edn, Diversion Books, New York, 2019.

4   L Gratton, 'How to do hybrid right', *Harvard Business Review*, May–June 2021, pp 66–74.

5   M Plummer, 'How are you protecting your high performers from burnout?', *Harvard Business Review*, 21 June 2018.

6   A Michel, 'Burnout and the brain', *Association for Psychological Science*, 29 January 2016.

7   M Pierce, H Hope, T Ford, S Hatch, M Hotopf, A John, E Kontopantelis, R Webb, S Wessely, S McManus & KM Abel, 'Mental health before and during the COVID-19 pandemic: a longitudinal probability sample survey of the UK population', *The Lancet Psychiatry*, vol 7, no 10, 2020, pp 883–892.

8   Australian Institute of Health and Welfare, *Mental Health Impact of COVID-19*, 2020, https://www.aihw.gov.au/getmedia/56ee7ea4-e211-49d8-85e4-853c01762aef/Mental-health-impact-of-COVID-19_1.pdf.

9   A Abbott, 'COVID's mental-health toll: how scientists are tracking a surge in depression', *Nature*, 3 February 2021, https://www.nature.com/articles/d41586-021-00175-z.

10 Team Asana, *Overcoming disruption in a disturbed world: Anatomy of Work Index*, 2021, available from https://blog.asana.com/2021/01/anz-anatomy-of-work-infographic/#close.

11 Springfox, *The Australian Workforce Response to COVID-19: A call for courage, connection and compassion*, 2020, https://www.springfox.com/wp-content/uploads/2020/11/Springfox-Report-The-Australian-Workforce-Response-to-COVID-19.pdf.

12 A De Smet, L Tegelberg, R Theunissen & T Vogel, 'Overcoming pandemic fatigue: how to reenergize organizations for the long run', McKinsey & Company, 25 November 2020, www.mckinsey.com.

13 C Maslach & MP Leiter, 'How to measure burnout accurately and ethically', *Harvard Business Review*, 19 March 2021.

14 CW Topp, SD Østergaard, S Søndergaard & P Bech, 'The WHO-5 Well-Being Index: a systematic review of the literature', *Psychotherapy and Psychosomatics*, vol 84, no 3, 2015, pp 167–76.

15 RE Boyatzis, D Goleman, U Dhar & K Osiri, 'Thrive and survive: assessing personal sustainability', *Consulting Psychology Journal: Practice and Research*, vol 73, no 1, 2021, pp 27–50.

16 D Rock, 'Managing with the brain in mind', *Strategy+Business*, 27 August 2009, no 56 (Autumn 2009).

17 RE Boyatzis et al, op cit.

18 WB Schaufeli, MP Leiter & C Maslach, 'Burnout: 35 years of research and practice', *Career Development International*, vol 14, no 3, 2008, pp 204–220.

19 World Health Organization, *International Classification of Diseases*, https://www.who.int/news/item/28-05-2019-burn-out-an-occupational-phenomenon-international-classification-of-diseases.

20 C Maslach & MP Leiter, op cit.

21 A Michel, op cit.

22 A Michel, op cit.

23 F Pega, B Náfrádi, N Momen, Y Ujita, KN Streicher, AM Prüss-Üstüna, et al, 'Global, regional, and national burdens of ischemic heart disease and stroke attributable to exposure to long working hours for 194 countries, 2000–2016: A systematic analysis from the WHO/ILO Joint Estimates of the Work-related Burden of Disease and Injury', *Environment International*, May 2021.

24 MP Leiter & C Maslach, 'Areas of worklife: a structured approach to organizational predictors of job burnout', in PL Perrewé & DC Ganster (eds), *Emotional and Physiological Processes and Positive Intervention Strategies*, 2003, pp 91–134.

25 MP Leiter & C Maslach, 'Conquering burnout', *Scientific American Mind*, vol 24, no 1, 2014, pp 30–35.

26 T Chamorro-Premuzic, 'To prevent burnout, hire better bosses', *Harvard Business Review*, 23 August 2019.

27 C Guthier, C Dormann & MC Voelkle, 'Reciprocal effects between job stressors and burnout: a continuous time meta-analysis of longitudinal studies', *Psychological Bulletin*, vol 146, no 12, 2020, pp 1146–1173.

28 MP Leiter & C Maslach, 'Conquering burnout', op cit.

29 T Chamorro-Premuzic, op cit.

30 RE Quinn, DP Fessell & SW Porges, 'How to keep your cool in high-stress situations', *Harvard Business Review*, 15 January 2021.

31 R Carucci, 'How to tell your boss you're burned out', *Harvard Business Review*, 5 January 2021.

32 S Sonnentag, L Venz & A Casper, 'Advances in recovery research: What have we learned? What should be done next?' *Journal of Occupational Health Psychology*, vol 22, no 3, 2017, pp 365–380.

33 RE Boyatzis et al, op cit.

34 MP Leiter & C Maslach, 'Conquering burnout', op cit.

35 L Eadicicco, 'Laurene Powell Jobs says people have been misinterpreting one of Steve Jobs' most famous quotes for years', *Business Insider Australia*, 29 February 2020.

36 J Moss, 'When passion leads to burnout', *Harvard Business Review*, 1 July 2019.

37 CD Ryff, *Psychological Wellbeing Scale*, available from https://sparqtools.org/mobility-measure/psychological-wellbeing-scale/.

38 S Sinek, *The Infinite Game*, Portfolio, New York, 2019.

39 PL Hill & NA Turiano, 'Purpose in life as a predictor of mortality across adulthood', *Psychological Science*, vol 25, no 7, pp 1482–86.

40 VJ Strecher, *Life on Purpose: How living for what matters most changes everything*, HarperOne, San Francisco, 2016.

41 RJ Vallerand, Y Paquet, FL Philippe & J Charest, 'On the role of passion for work in burnout: a process model', *Journal of Personality*, vol 78, no 1, 2010, pp 289–312.

42 G Ward, H Collins, MI Norton & AV Whillans, *Work Values Shape the Relationship between Stress and (Un)Happiness*, Working Paper 21-044, 21 September 2020, https://www.hbs.edu/faculty/Publication%20Files/21-044_f5a41dc5-0489-46c1-9338-d93165f09434.pdf.

43 CA Baker, 'Between stimulus and response, there is a space', Medium.com, 25 January 2018, https://medium.com/@colemanabaker/between-stimulus-and-response-there-is-a-space-ad5261e3c74e.

44 SC Hayes, *A Liberated Mind: The essential guide to ACT*, Vermillion, London, 2019.

45 S David, *Emotional Agility: Get unstuck, embrace change, and thrive in work and life*, Penguin Books, London, 2016.

46 J Garvey Berger, *Unlocking Leadership Mindtraps: How to thrive in complexity*, Stanford University Press, Stanford, California, 2019.

47 T Kashdan & R Biswas-Diener, *The Power of Negative Emotion: How anger, guilt and self doubt are essential to success and fulfillment*, Oneworld Publications, London, 2015.

48 C Kidd & BY Hayden, 'The psychology and neuroscience of curiosity', *Neuron*, vol 88, no 3, 2015, pp 449–60.

49 J Bersin, 'New research shows "heavy learners" more confident, successful, and happy at work', 9 November 2018, https://www.linkedin.com/pulse/want-happy-work-spend-time-learning-josh-bersin.

50 C McChesney, S Covey & J Huling, *The 4 Disciplines of Execution: Achieving your wildly important goals*, Free Press, New York, 2012.

51 T Neeley, *Remote Work Revolution: Succeeding from anywhere*, Harper Business, New York, 2021.

52 A Wrzesniewski, JM Berg & JE Dutton, 'Managing yourself: turn the job you have into the job you want', *Harvard Business Review*, June 2010.

53 R Cenciotti, G Alessandri & L Borgogni, 'Psychological capital and career success over time: the mediating role of job crafting', *Journal of Leadership & Organizational Studies*, vol 24, no 3, 2017, pp 372–384

54 F Luthans & CM Youssef-Morgan, 'Psychological capital: an evidence-based positive approach', *Annual Review of Organizational Psychology and Organizational Behavior*, vol 4, no 1, 2017, pp 339–366.

55 SG Rogelberg, 'The surprising science behind successful remote meetings', *MIT Sloan Management Review*, 21 May 2020.

56 SG Rogelberg, 'Why your meetings stink – and what to do about it', *Harvard Business Review*, January–February 2019.

57 C McChesney et al, op cit.

58 T Neeley, op cit.

59 M Blanding, 'Succeeding in the new work-from-anywhere world', Harvard Business School *Working Knowledge*, 23 March 2021, https://hbswk.hbs.edu/item/succeeding-in-the-new-work-from-anywhere-world.

60 Ibid.

61 C Reidl, & AW Woolley, '"Bursty" communication can help remote teams thrive', *Behavioral Scientist*, 29 May 2018.

62 R Heifetz, M Linsky & A Grashow, *The Practice of Adaptive Leadership: Tools and tactics for changing your organization and the world*, Harvard Business Press, Boston, Massachusetts, 2009.

63 D Goleman & RJ Davidson, *The Science of Meditation: How to change your brain, mind and body*, Penguin Random House UK, London, 2017.

64 R Harris, *ACT Made Simple*, New Harbinger Publications, Inc, Oakland, California, 2009.

65 C Newport, *Deep Work: Rules for focused success in a distracted world*, Piatkus Books, London, 2016.

66 E Bernstein & B Waber, 'The truth about open offices', *Harvard Business Review*, November–December 2019.

67 E Bernstein, J Shore & D Lazer, 'Improving the rhythm of your collaboration', MIT Sloan Management Review, 10 September 2019.

68 W Wood, *Good Habits, Bad Habits: The science of making positive changes that stick*, Pan MacMillan, 2019.

69 W Wood, op cit.

70 Ibid.

71 Ibid.

72 J Hyun, MJ Sliwinski & JM Smyth, 'Waking up on the wrong side of the bed: the effects of stress anticipation on working memory in daily life', *The Journals of Gerontology: Series B*, vol 74, no 1, 2019, pp. 38–46.

73 S Sonnentag, K Eck, C Fritz & J Kühnel, 'Morning reattachment to work and work engagement through the day: a look at day-level mediators', *Journal of Management*, vol 46, no 8, 2019, pp 1408–1435.

74 S Achor & M Gielan, 'Resilience is about how you recharge, not how you endure', *Harvard Business Review*, 24 June 2016, https://hbr.org/2016/06/resilience-is-about-how-you-recharge-not-how-you-endure.

75 S Sonnentag, 'Psychological detachment from work during leisure time', *Current Directions in Psychological Science*, vol 21, no 2, 2012, pp 114–118.

76 R Boyatzis & A McKee, *Resonant Leadership: Renewing yourself and connecting with others through mindfulness, hope and compassion*, Harvard Business School Press, Boston, Massachusetts, 2005.

77 AJ Cuddy, M Kohut & J Neffinger, 'Connect, then lead', *Harvard Business Review*, July–August 2013, pp 55–61.

78 AJC Cuddy, ST Fiske & P Glick, 'Warmth and competence as universal dimensions of social perception: the stereotype content model and the BIAS map', in MP Zanna (ed), *Advances in Experimental Social Psychology*, vol 40, 2008, pp 61–149.

79 AE Abele & B Wojciszke, 'Communal and agentic content in social cognition', *Advances in Experimental Social Psychology*, vol 50, 2014, pp 195–255.

80 CF Bilton & AL Pincus, *Construction and validation of the Interpersonal Influence Tactics Circumplex (IIT-C) Scales*, Assessment, 2019, pp 11–18.

81 CS Reina, KM Rogers, SJ Peterson, K Byron & PW Hom, 'Quitting the boss? The role of manager influence tactics and employee emotional engagement in voluntary turnover', *Journal of Leadership & Organizational Studies*, vol 25, no 1, pp 5–18.

82 T Sharot, *The Influential Mind: What the brain reveals about our power to change others*, Little, Brown, London, 2017.

83 Ibid.

84 G Yukl, CF Seifert & C Chavez, 'Validation of the extended Influence Behavior Questionnaire', *The Leadership Quarterly*, vol 19, no 5, 2008, pp 609–621.

85 D Goleman, 'Leadership that gets results', *Harvard Business Review*, March–April 2000, pp 78–90.

86 Ibid.

87 JC Maxwell, *Developing the Leaders Around You: How to help others reach their full potential*, Nelson Business, 1995.

88 AC Edmondson, *The Fearless Organization: Creating psychological safety in the workplace for learning, innovation, and growth*, John Wiley & Sons, Hoboken, New Jersey, 2018.

89 RE Boyatzis, ML Smith & E Van Oosten, *Helping People Change: Coaching with compassion for lifelong learning and growth*, Harvard Business Review Press, Boston, Massachusetts, 2019.

90 TM Amabile & SJ Kramer, *The Progress Principle: Using small wins to ignite joy, engagement, and creativity at work*, Harvard Business Review Press, Boston, Massachusetts, 2011.

91 T Huston, *Let's talk: Make effective feedback your superpower*, Penguin, 2021.

92 Ibid.

93 T Huston, 'When you need to give tough feedback, forget Zoom and pick up the phone', *Fast Company*, 8 October 2020.

94 T Huston, *Let's talk: Make effective feedback your superpower*, Penguin, 2021.

95 J Schleckser, 'The 5 levels of delegation you need to know to lead well', *Inc.*, 7 November 2017.

96 PJ Zak, 'Why your brain loves good storytelling', *Harvard Business Review*, 28 October 2014.

97 Ibid.

98 PJ Zak, 'The neuroscience of trust', *Harvard Business Review*, January–February 2017, pp 85–90.

99 G Dolan & Y Naidu, *Hooked: How leaders conspire, engage and inspire with storytelling*, John Wiley & Sons, Australia, Melbourne, 2013

100 AJC Cuddy, *Presence: Bringing your boldest self to your biggest challenges*, The Orion Publishing Group, London, 2015.

101 BL Halpern & K Lubar, *Leadership Presence*, Gotham Books, New York, 2003.

102 Ibid.

INDEX

ABOUT THE AUTHOR

Dr Karen Morley helps leaders get more impact with less effort. The global pandemic has increased the burdens on high-achieving leaders, and her focus is on helping leaders to reset the way they work. She helps leaders to challenge overwork, rediscover their purpose and rebalance their life to beat chronic stress and burnout.

Karen has held executive leadership roles and is also a self-declared high achiever; her approach is closely informed by these experiences.

She's a registered psychologist and brings her fascination with emerging neuroscience and social psychology research to give leaders insight into what really works. She is deeply committed to making behavioural change easier and provides practical takeaways that leaders can readily turn into new habits.

Karen is an experienced executive coach working with leaders in organisations such as Allens, BHP, Broadspectrum, Bunnings, Commonwealth Bank, Coles, CSL, Downer, Essential Energy, Fulton Hogan, Guild Group, Hassell, Kmart, Latitude Financial Services, Lendlease, L'Oréal, Medibank, Melbourne Water, Monash Health, NAWO, Officeworks, Orica, QBE, RACV, SBS, Target, TerryWhite Chemmart, the University of Melbourne and the Victoria State Government Departments of Education and Training, Health and Human Services, Justice and Community Safety, and Jobs, Precincts and Regions.

She is an Opinion Columnist with *CEOWORLD* magazine and an Honorary Fellow of the University of Melbourne.

WORK WITH KAREN

Karen's services include:

- FlexAbility Coaching to reset your purpose, balance and focus
- Executive Coaching to increase your leadership influence
- Peer-based Coaching Circles to achieve more power through collaboration
- Inclusive Leadership Coaching to embed inclusion and belonging practices.

Find out more about how Karen can work with you or your organisation by visiting **www.karenmorley.com.au**, emailing **kmorley@karenmorley.com.au** or calling **+61 438 215 391**. For regular insights, follow Karen on Linkedin at **www.linkedin. com/in/karenmorley**.

ALSO BY KAREN MORLEY

Lead Like a Coach is for leaders who care about the people they lead; care about their own success; and want to make a positive impact on their stakeholders, their families and their communities. It is packed with practical strategies and case studies making it easy for anyone to start to lead like a coach.

Bias might be built in to how our brains work, but that doesn't make it acceptable. In *Beat Gender Bias*, Dr Karen Morley outlines an approach for minimising the impact of bias in organisations with Bias Busters – specific actions you can take with the goal of making it easier to notice, talk about and overcome bias.

For more information, visit www.majorstreet.com.au